Jung Lexicon

Marie-Louise von Franz, Honorary Patron

**Studies in Jungian Psychology
by Jungian Analysts**

Daryl Sharp, General Editor

JUNG LEXICON

A Primer of
Terms & Concepts

DARYL SHARP

To Edward F. Edinger, who keeps me honest;
to Vicki, who helped me iron out the wrinkles;
and to Rachel, who holds me to my truth.

Also by Daryl Sharp in this series:
The Secret Raven: Conflict and Transformation (#1, 1980)
Personality Types: Jung's Model of Typology (#31, 1987)
The Survival Papers: Anatomy of a Midlife Crisis (#35, 1988)
Dear Gladys: The Survival Papers, Book 2 (#37, 1989)

Canadian Cataloguing in Publication Data

Sharp, Daryl, 1936-
Jung lexicon

(Studies in Jungian psychology by Jungian analysts; 47)

Includes bibliographical references.

ISBN 0-919123-48-1

1. Jung, C.G. (Carl Gustav), 1875-1961—Dictionaries, indexes, etc.
2. Psychoanalysis—Dictionaries.
I. Title. II. Series.

BF173.J85S4 1991   150.19'54'03   C90-095257-1

INNER CITY BOOKS
Box 1271, Station Q, Toronto, Canada M4T 2P4
Telephone (416) 927-0355
FAX 416-924-1814

Honorary Patron: Marie-Louise von Franz.
Publisher and General Editor: Daryl Sharp.
Senior Editor: Victoria Cowan.

INNER CITY BOOKS was founded in 1980 to promote the
understanding and practical application of the work of C.G. Jung.

Index by the author.

Printed and bound in Canada by
University of Toronto Press Incorporated

Contents

See final page for descriptions of other Inner City Books

The opus consists of three parts: insight, endurance, and action. Psychology is needed only in the first part, but in the second and third parts moral strength plays the predominant role.

—Jung, *Letters.*

He who would be initiated into this art and secret wisdom must put away the vice of arrogance, must be devout, righteous, deep-witted, humane towards his fellows, of a cheerful countenance and a happy disposition, and respectful withal. Likewise he must be an observer of the eternal secrets that are revealed to him.

—*Ars chemica* (1566), quoted by Jung in
"Psychology of the Transference."

Jung at the age of 75

Preface

C.G. Jung died in 1961, without ever having presented a systematic summary of his psychology. For the past thirty years his ideas have been explained, explored and amplified by thousands of others, with varying results.

Jung Lexicon takes the reader to the source. It was designed for those seeking an understanding of relevant terms and concepts as they were used by Jung himself. There are choice extracts from Jung's *Collected Works,* but no references to other writers.

Jung Lexicon is not a critique or defence of Jung's thought, but a guide to its richness and an illustration of the broad scope and interrelationship of his interests.

Informed by a close reading of Jung's major writings, *Jung Lexicon* contains a comprehensive overview of the basic principles of Jungian psychology. The implications and practical application of Jung's ideas are well covered by other volumes in this series.

Note on Usage

A word that appears in **bold** type under a main heading directs the reader to another entry in this book. All main entries are flagged in this way in the comprehensive index at the end, which will further lead the reader to the many different contexts in which Jung used the terms and concepts presented here.

The designation CW in the footnotes refers to the twenty volumes of Jung's *Collected Works*. The titles of the individual volumes are given in the Bibliography.

Abaissement du niveau mental. A lowering of the level of consciousness, a mental and emotional condition experienced as "loss of soul." (See also **depression.**)

> It is a slackening of the tensity of consciousness, which might be compared to a low barometric reading, presaging bad weather. The tonus has given way, and this is felt subjectively as listlessness, moroseness, and depression. One no longer has any wish or courage to face the tasks of the day. One feels like lead, because no part of one's body seems willing to move, and this is due to the fact that one no longer has any disposable energy. . . . The listlessness and paralysis of will can go so far that the whole personality falls apart, so to speak, and consciousness loses its unity . . . .
>
> *Abaissement du niveau mental* can be the result of physical and mental fatigue, bodily illness, violent emotions, and shock, of which the last has a particularly deleterious effect on one's self-assurance. The *abaissement* always has a restrictive influence on the personality as a whole. It reduces one's self-confidence and the spirit of enterprise, and, as a result of increasing egocentricity, narrows the mental horizon.[1]

Abreaction. A method of becoming conscious of repressed emotional reactions through the retelling and reliving of a traumatic experience. (See also **cathartic method.**)

After some initial interest in "trauma theory," Jung abandoned abreaction (together with suggestion) as an effective tool in the therapy of neurosis.

> I soon discovered that, though traumata of clearly aetiological significance were occasionally present, the majority of them appeared very improbable. Many traumata were so unimportant, even so normal, that they could be regarded at most as a pretext for the neurosis. But what especially aroused my criticism was the fact that not a few traumata were simply inventions of fantasy and had never happened at all. . . . I could no longer imagine that repeated experiences of a fantastically exaggerated or entirely fictitious trauma had a different therapeutic value from a suggestion procedure.[2]

---

[1] "Concerning Rebirth," CW 9i, pars. 213f.
[2] "Some Crucial Points in Psychoanalysis," CW 4, par. 582.

The belief, the self-confidence, perhaps also the devotion with which the analyst does his work, are far more important to the patient (imponderabilia though they may be), than the rehearsing of old traumata.[3]

Abstraction. A form of mental activity by which a conscious content is freed from its association with irrelevant elements, similar to the process of **differentiation.** (Compare **empathy.**)

> Abstraction is an activity pertaining to the psychological functions in general. There is an abstract thinking, just as there is abstract feeling, sensation, and intuition. Abstract thinking singles out the rational, logical qualities of a given content from its intellectually irrelevant components. Abstract feeling does the same with a content characterized by its feeling-values .... Abstract sensation would be aesthetic as opposed to sensuous sensation, and abstract intuition would be symbolic as opposed to fantastic intuition.[4]

Jung related abstraction to introversion (analogous to empathy and extraversion).

> I visualize the process of abstraction as a withdrawal of libido from the object, as a backflow of value from the object into a subjective, abstract content. For me, therefore, abstraction amounts to an energic *devaluation of the object.* In other words, abstraction is an introverting movement of libido.[5]

To the extent that its purpose is to break the object's hold on the subject, abstraction is an attempt to rise above the primitive state of *participation mystique.*

Active imagination. A method of assimilating unconscious contents (dreams, fantasies, etc.) through some form of self-expression. (See also **transcendent function.**)

The object of active imagination is to give a voice to sides of the personality (particularly the anima/animus and the shadow) that are normally not heard, thereby establishing a line of communication be-

---

[3] Ibid., par. 584.

[4] "Definitions," CW 6, par. 678.

[5] Ibid., par. 679.

tween consciousness and the unconscious. Even when the end products—drawing, painting, writing, sculpture, dance, music, etc.—are not interpreted, something goes on between creator and creation that contributes to a transformation of consciousness.

The first stage of active imagination is like dreaming with open eyes. It can take place spontaneously or be artificially induced.

> In the latter case you choose a dream, or some other fantasy-image, and concentrate on it by simply catching hold of it and looking at it. You can also use a bad mood as a starting-point, and then try to find out what sort of fantasy-image it will produce, or what image expresses this mood. You then fix this image in the mind by concentrating your attention. Usually it will alter, as the mere fact of contemplating it animates it. The alterations must be carefully noted down all the time, for they reflect the psychic processes in the unconscious background, which appear in the form of images consisting of conscious memory material. In this way conscious and unconscious are united, just as a waterfall connects above and below.[6]

The second stage, beyond simply observing the images, involves a conscious participation in them, the honest evaluation of what they mean about oneself, and a morally and intellectually binding commitment to act on the insights. This is a transition from a merely perceptive or aesthetic attitude to one of judgment.

> Although, to a certain extent, he looks on from outside, impartially, he is also an acting and suffering figure in the drama of the psyche. This recognition is absolutely necessary and marks an important advance. So long as he simply looks at the pictures he is like the foolish Parsifal, who forgot to ask the vital question because he was not aware of his own participation in the action.[7] . . . But if you recognize your own involvement you yourself must enter into the process with your personal reactions, just as if you were one of the fantasy figures, or rather, as if the drama being enacted before your eyes were real.[8]

---

[6] "The Conjunction," CW 14, par. 706.

[7] An allusion to the medieval Grail legend. The question Parsifal failed to ask was, "Whom does the Grail serve?"

[8] "The Conjunction," CW 14, par. 753.

The judging attitude implies a voluntary involvement in those fantasy-processes which compensate the individual and—in particular—the collective situation of consciousness. The avowed purpose of this involvement is to integrate the statements of the unconscious, to assimilate their compensatory content, and thereby produce a whole meaning which alone makes life worth living and, for not a few people, possible at all.[9]

Adaptation. The process of coming to terms with the external world, on the one hand, and with one's own unique psychological characteristics on the other. (See also **neurosis.**)

> Before [individuation] can be taken as a goal, the educational aim of adaptation to the necessary minimum of collective norms must first be attained. If a plant is to unfold its specific nature to the full, it must first be able to grow in the soil in which it is planted.[10]

> The constant flow of life again and again demands fresh adaptation. Adaptation is never achieved once and for all.[11]

> Man is not a machine in the sense that he can consistently maintain the same output of work. He can meet the demands of outer necessity in an ideal way only if he is also adapted to his own inner world, that is, if he is in harmony with himself. Conversely, he can only adapt to his inner world and achieve harmony with himself when he is adapted to the environmental conditions.[12]

The transition from child to adult initially entails an increasing adaptation to the outer world. When the libido meets an obstacle to progression, there is an accumulation of energy that normally gives rise to increased efforts to overcome the obstacle. But if the obstacle proves insurmountable, the stored-up energy regresses to an earlier mode of adaptation. This in turn activates infantile fantasies and wishes, and necessitates the need to adapt to the inner world.

> The best examples of such regressions are found in hysterical cases where a disappointment in love or marriage has precipitated a neuro-

---

[9] Ibid., par. 756.
[10] "Definitions," CW 6, par. 761.
[11] "The Transcendent Function," CW 8, par. 143.
[12] "On Psychic Energy," ibid., par. 75.

sis. There we find those well-known digestive disorders, loss of appetite, dyspeptic symptoms of all sorts, etc. . . . . [typically accompanied by] a regressive revival of reminiscences from the distant past. We then find a reactivation of the parental imagos, of the Oedipus complex. Here the events of early infancy—never before important—suddenly become so. They have been regressively reactivated. Remove the obstacle from the path of life and this whole system of infantile fantasies at once breaks down and becomes as inactive and ineffective as before.[13]

In his model of typology, Jung described two substantially different modes of adaptation, introversion and extraversion. He also linked failures in adaptation to the outbreak of neurosis.

The psychological trouble in neurosis, and the neurosis itself, can be formulated as *an act of adaptation that has failed.*[14]

Affect. Emotional reactions marked by physical symptoms and disturbances in thinking. (See also **complex** and **feeling.**)
Affect is invariably a sign that a complex has been activated.

Affects occur usually where adaptation is weakest, and at the same time they reveal the reason for its weakness, namely a certain degree of inferiority and the existence of a lower level of personality. On this lower level with its uncontrolled or scarcely controlled emotions one . . . [is] singularly incapable of moral judgment.[15]

Ambivalence. A state of mind where every attitude or anticipated course of action is counterbalanced by its opposite. (See also **conflict** and **opposites.**)
Ambivalence is associated in general with the influence of unconscious complexes, and in particular with the psychological functions when they have not been differentiated.

Amplification. A method of association based on the comparative study of mythology, religion and fairy tales, used in the interpretation of images in dreams and drawings.

---

13 "Psychoanalysis and Neurosis," CW4, par. 569.
14 Ibid., par. 574 (italics in original).
15 "The Shadow," *Aion,* CW 9ii, par. 15.

Analysis, Jungian. A form of therapy specializing in neurosis, aimed at bringing unconscious contents to consciousness; also called analytic therapy, based on the school of thought developed by C.G. Jung called analytical (or complex) psychology.

[Analysis] is only a means for removing the stones from the path of development, and not a method . . . of putting things into the patient that were not there before. It is better to renounce any attempt to give direction, and simply try to throw into relief everything that the analysis brings to light, so that the patient can see it clearly and be able to draw suitable conclusions. Anything he has not acquired himself he will not believe in the long run, and what he takes over from authority merely keeps him infantile. He should rather be put in a position to take his own life in hand. The art of analysis lies in following the patient on all his erring ways and so gathering his strayed sheep together.[16]

There is a widespread prejudice that analysis is something like a "cure," to which one submits for a time and is then discharged healed. That is a layman's error left over from the early days of psychoanalysis. Analytical treatment could be described as a readjustment of psychological attitude achieved with the help of the doctor. . . . [But] there is no change that is unconditionally valid over a long period of time.[17]

Jung initially made a distinction between *analysis of the unconscious*[18] and *anamnestic analysis.* The latter is concerned primarily with contents of consciousness already available or easily brought to mind, and with supporting or strengthening the ego. The unconscious is a factor only indirectly.

It consists in a careful anamnesis or reconstruction of the historical development of the neurosis. The material elicited in this way is a

---

[16] "Some Crucial Points in Psychoanalysis," CW 4, par. 643.

[17] "The Transcendent Function," CW 8, par. 142.

[18] Jung deliberately used this expression instead of "psychoanalysis": "I wish to leave that term entirely to the Freudians. What they understand by psychoanalysis is no mere technique, but a method which is dogmatically bound up with and based upon Freud's sexual theory. When Freud publicly declared that psychoanalysis and his sexual theory were indissolubly wedded, I was obliged to strike out on a different path." ("Analytical Psychology and Education," CW 17, par. 180)

more or less coherent sequence of facts told to the doctor by the patient, so far as he can remember them. He naturally omits many details which either seem unimportant to him or which he has forgotten. The experienced analyst who knows the usual course of neurotic development will put questions which help the patient to fill in some of the gaps. Very often this procedure by itself is of great therapeutic value, as it enables the patient to understand the chief factors of his neurosis and may eventually bring him to a decisive change of attitude.[19]

In addition to the favourable effect produced by the realization of previously unconscious connections, it is usual for the doctor to give some good advice, or encouragement, or even a reproof.[20]

Analysis of the unconscious begins when conscious material has been exhausted and there is still no satisfactory resolution of the neurosis; it requires an ego strong enough to deal directly with unconscious material, particularly dreams. Jung believed that analysis in this sense was particularly suited to psychological problems in the second half of life, but even then he expressed caution.

Consistent support of the conscious attitude has in itself a high therapeutic value and not infrequently serves to bring about satisfactory results. It would be a dangerous prejudice to imagine that analysis of the unconscious is the one and only panacea which should therefore be employed in every case. It is rather like a surgical operation and we should only resort to the knife when other methods have failed. So long as it does not obtrude itself the unconscious is best left alone.[21]

In his analytic work, Jung shunned diagnosis and prognosis. He used no systematic technique or method. His aim was to approach each case with a minimum of prior assumptions, although he acknowledged that the personality and psychological disposition of the analyst made complete objectivity impossible.

The ideal would naturally be to have no assumptions at all. But this is impossible even if one exercises the most rigorous self-criticism,

---

[19] "Analytical Psychology and Education," ibid., par. 177.
[20] Ibid., par. 178.
[21] "The Psychology of the Transference," CW 16, par. 381.

for one is *oneself* the biggest of all one's assumptions, and the one with the gravest consequences. Try as we may to have no assumptions and to use no ready-made methods, the assumption that I myself am will determine my method: as I am, so will I proceed.[22]

Jung also insisted that those training to be analysts must have a thorough personal analysis.

> We have learned to place in the foreground the personality of the doctor himself as a curative or harmful factor; . . . what is now demanded is his own transformation—the self-education of the educator. . . . The doctor can no longer evade his own difficulty by treating the difficulties of others: the man who suffers from a running abscess is not fit to perform a surgical operation.[23]

Anima. The inner feminine side of a man. (See also **animus, Eros, Logos** and **soul-image**.)

The anima is both a personal complex and an archetypal image of woman in the male psyche. It is an unconscious factor incarnated anew in every male child, and is responsible for the mechanism of projection. Initially identified with the personal mother, the anima is later experienced not only in other women but as a pervasive influence in a man's life.

> The anima is the *archetype of life itself.*[24]

> There is [in man] an imago not only of the mother but of the daughter, the sister, the beloved, the heavenly goddess, and the chthonic Baubo. Every mother and every beloved is forced to become the carrier and embodiment of this omnipresent and ageless image, which corresponds to the deepest reality in a man. It belongs to him, this perilous image of Woman; she stands for the loyalty which in the interests of life he must sometimes forego; she is the much needed compensation for the risks, struggles, sacrifices that all end in disappointment; she is the solace for all the bitterness of life. And, at the same time, she is the great illusionist, the seductress, who draws him into life with her Maya—and not only into life's reasonable and

---

22 "Appendix," ibid., par. 543.
23 "Problems of Modern Psychotherapy," ibid., par. 172.
24 "Archetypes of the Collective Unconscious," CW 9i, par. 66.

useful aspects, but into its frightful paradoxes and ambivalences where good and evil, success and ruin, hope and despair, counterbalance one another. Because she is his greatest danger she demands from a man his greatest, and if he has it in him she will receive it.[25]

The anima is personified in dreams by images of women ranging from seductress to spiritual guide. It is associated with the eros principle, hence a man's anima development is reflected in how he relates to women. Within his own psyche, the anima functions as his soul, influencing his ideas, attitudes and emotions.

The anima is not the soul in the dogmatic sense, not an *anima rationalis*, which is a philosophical conception, but a natural archetype that satisfactorily sums up all the statements of the unconscious, of the primitive mind, of the history of language and religion. . . . It is always the *a priori* element in [a man's] moods, reactions, impulses, and whatever else is spontaneous in psychic life.[26]

The anima . . . . intensifies, exaggerates, falsifies, and mythologizes all emotional relations with his work and with other people of both sexes. The resultant fantasies and entanglements are all her doing. When the anima is strongly constellated, she softens the man's character and makes him touchy, irritable, moody, jealous, vain, and unadjusted.[27]

As an inner personality, the anima is complementary to the persona and stands in a compensatory relationship to it.

The persona, the ideal picture of a man as he should be, is inwardly compensated by feminine weakness, and as the individual outwardly plays the strong man, so he becomes inwardly a woman, i.e., the anima, for it is the anima that reacts to the persona. But because the inner world is dark and invisible . . . and because a man is all the less capable of conceiving his weaknesses the more he is identified with the persona, the persona's counterpart, the anima, remains completely in the dark and is at once projected, so that our hero comes under the heel of his wife's slipper.[28]

25 "The Syzygy: Anima and Animus," CW 9ii, par. 24
26 "Archetypes of the Collective Unconscious," CW 9i, par. 57.
27 "Concerning the Archetypes and the Anima Concept," ibid., par. 144.
28 "Anima and Animus," CW 7, par. 309.

Hence the character of the anima can generally be deduced from that of the persona; all those qualities absent from the outer attitude will be found in the inner.

> The tyrant tormented by bad dreams, gloomy forebodings, and inner fears is a typical figure. Outwardly ruthless, harsh, and unapproachable, he jumps inwardly at every shadow, is at the mercy of every mood, as though he were the feeblest and most impressionable of men. Thus his anima contains all those fallible human qualities his persona lacks. If the persona is intellectual, the anima will certainly be sentimental.[29]

Similarly, where a man identifies with the persona, he is in effect possessed by the anima, with attendant symptoms.

> Identity with the persona automatically leads to an unconscious identity with the anima because, when the ego is not differentiated from the persona, it can have no conscious relation to the unconscious processes. Consequently it *is* these processes, it is identical with them. Anyone who is himself his outward role will infallibly succumb to the inner processes; he will either frustrate his outward role by absolute inner necessity or else reduce it to absurdity, by a process of enantiodromia. He can no longer keep to his individual way, and his life runs into one deadlock after another. Moreover, the anima is inevitably projected upon a real object, with which he gets into a relation of almost total dependence.[30]

Jung distinguished four broad stages of the anima, analogous to levels of the Eros cult described in the late classical period. He personified them as Eve, Helen, Mary and Sophia.[31]

In the first stage, Eve, the anima is indistinguishable from the personal mother. The man cannot function well without a close tie to a woman. In the second stage, personified in the historical figure of Helen of Troy, the anima is a collective and ideal sexual image ("All is dross that is not Helen"—Marlowe). The third stage, Mary, manifests in religious feelings and a capacity for lasting relationships. In the fourth stage, as Sophia (called Wisdom in the Bible), a man's

---

29 "Definitions," CW 6, par. 804.
30 Ibid., par. 807.
31 "The Psychology of the Transference," CW 16, par. 361.

anima functions as a guide to the inner life, mediating to consciousness the contents of the unconscious. She cooperates in the search for meaning and is the creative muse in an artist's life.

Ideally, a man's anima proceeds naturally through these stages as he grows older. In fact, as an archetypal life force, the anima manifests in whatever shape or form is necessary to compensate the dominant conscious attitude.

So long as the anima is unconscious, everything she stands for is projected. Most commonly, because of the initially close tie between the anima and the protective mother-imago, this projection falls on the partner, with predictable results.

> [A man's] ideal of marriage is so arranged that his wife has to take over the magical role of the mother. Under the cloak of the ideally exclusive marriage he is really seeking his mother's protection, and thus he plays into the hands of his wife's possessive instincts. His fear of the dark incalculable power of the unconscious gives his wife an illegitimate authority over him, and forges such a dangerously close union that the marriage is permanently on the brink of explosion from internal tension.[32]

No matter where a man is in terms of psychological development, he is always prone to see aspects of his anima, his soul, in an actual woman. The same is true of the animus. Their personal aspects may be integrated and their significance understood, but their essential nature cannot be exhausted.

> Though the effects of anima and animus can be made conscious, they themselves are factors transcending consciousness and beyond the reach of perception and volition. Hence they remain autonomous despite the integration of their contents, and for this reason they should be borne constantly in mind.[33]

The psychological priority in the first half of life is for a man to free himself from the anima fascination of the mother. In later life, the lack of a conscious relationship with the anima is attended by symptoms characteristic of "loss of soul."

---

[32] "Anima and Animus," CW 7, par. 316.
[33] "The Syzygy: Anima and Animus," CW 9ii, par. 40.

Younger people . . . can bear even the total loss of the anima without injury. The important thing at this stage is for a man to be a
man. . . .

After the middle of life, however, permanent loss of the anima
means a diminution of vitality, of flexibility, and of human kind-
ness. The result, as a rule, is premature rigidity, crustiness, stereo-
typy, fanatical one-sidedness, obstinacy, pedantry, or else resigna-
tion, weariness, sloppiness, irresponsibility, and finally a childish
ramollissement [petulance] with a tendency to alcohol.[34]

One way for a man to become familiar with the nature of his anima
is through the method of active imagination. This is done by personi-
fying her as an autonomous personality, asking her questions and at-
tending to the response.

I mean this as an actual technique. . . . The art of it consists only in
allowing our invisible partner to make herself heard, in putting the
mechanism of expression momentarily at her disposal, without being overcome by the distaste one naturally feels at playing such an
apparently ludicrous game with oneself, or by doubts as to the gen-
uineness of the voice of one's interlocutor.[35]

Jung suggested that if the encounter with the shadow is the
"apprentice-piece" in a man's development, then coming to terms
with the anima is the "master-piece."[36] The goal is her transformation from a troublesome adversary into a function of relationship
between consciousness and the unconscious. Jung called this "the
conquest of the anima as an autonomous complex."

With the attainment of this goal it becomes possible to disengage
the ego from all its entanglements with collectivity and the collective unconscious. Through this process the anima forfeits the daemonic power of an autonomous complex; she can no longer exercise
the power of possession, since she is depotentiated. She is no longer
the guardian of treasures unknown; no longer Kundry, daemonic
Messenger of the Grail, half divine and half animal; no longer is the
soul to be called "Mistress," but a psychological function of an intu-

34 "Concerning the Archetypes and the Anima Concept," CW 9i, par. 146f.
35 "Anima and Animus," CW 7, pars. 323f.
36 "Archetypes of the Collective Unconscious," CW 9i, par. 61.

itive nature, akin to what the primitives mean when they say, "He has gone into the forest to talk with the spirits" or "My snake spoke with me" or, in the mythological language of infancy, "A little bird told me."[37]

Animus. The inner masculine side of a woman. (See also **anima, Eros, Logos** and **soul-image**.)

Like the anima in a man, the animus is both a personal complex and an archetypal image.

> Woman is compensated by a masculine element and therefore her unconscious has, so to speak, a masculine imprint. This results in a considerable psychological difference between men and women, and accordingly I have called the projection-making factor in women the animus, which means mind or spirit. The animus corresponds to the paternal Logos just as the anima corresponds to the maternal Eros.[38]

> The animus is the deposit, as it were, of all woman's ancestral experiences of man—and not only that, he is also a creative and procreative being, not in the sense of masculine creativity, but in the sense that he brings forth something we might call . . . the spermatic word.[39]

Whereas the anima in a man functions as his soul, a woman's animus is more like an unconscious mind.[40] It manifests negatively in fixed ideas, collective opinions and unconscious, *a priori* assumptions that lay claim to absolute truth. In a woman who is identified with the animus (called animus-possession), Eros generally takes second place to Logos.

> A woman possessed by the animus is always in danger of losing her femininity.[41]

> No matter how friendly and obliging a woman's Eros may be, no logic on earth can shake her if she is ridden by the animus. . . . [A

---

[37] "The Mana-Personality," CW 7, par. 374.

[38] "The Syzygy: Anima and Animus," CW 9ii, pars. 28f.

[39] "Anima and Animus," CW 7, par. 336.

[40] At times Jung also referred to the animus as a woman's soul. See **soul** and **soul-image**.

[41] "Anima and Animus," CW 7, par. 337.

man] is unaware that this highly dramatic situation would instantly come to a banal and unexciting end if he were to quit the field and let a second woman carry on the battle (his wife, for instance, if she herself is not the fiery war horse). This sound idea seldom or never occurs to him, because no man can converse with an animus for five minutes without becoming the victim of his own anima.[42]

The animus becomes a helpful psychological factor when a woman can tell the difference between the ideas generated by this autonomous complex and what she herself really thinks.

Like the anima, the animus too has a positive aspect. Through the figure of the father he expresses not only conventional opinion but—equally—what we call "spirit," philosophical or religious ideas in particular, or rather the attitude resulting from them. Thus the animus is a psychopomp, a mediator between the conscious and the unconscious and a personification of the latter.[43]

Jung described four stages of animus development in a woman. He first appears in dreams and fantasy as the embodiment of physical power, an athlete, muscle man or thug. In the second stage, the animus provides her with initiative and the capacity for planned action. He is behind a woman's desire for independence and a career of her own. In the next stage, the animus is the "word," often personified in dreams as a professor or clergyman. In the fourth stage, the animus is the incarnation of spiritual meaning. On this highest level, like the anima as Sophia, the animus mediates between a woman's conscious mind and the unconscious. In mythology this aspect of the animus appears as Hermes, messenger of the gods; in dreams he is a helpful guide.

Any of these aspects of the animus can be projected onto a man. As with the projected anima, this can lead to unrealistic expectations and acrimony in relationships.

Like the anima, the animus is a jealous lover. He is adept at putting, in place of the real man, an opinion about him, the exceedingly disputable grounds for which are never submitted to criticism. Animus opinions are invariably collective, and they override individuals and

---

42 "The Syzygy: Anima and Animus," CW 9ii, par. 29.
43 Ibid., par. 33.

individual judgments in exactly the same way as the anima thrusts her emotional anticipations and projections between man and wife.[44]

The existence of the contrasexual complexes means that in any relationship between a man and a woman there are at least four personalities involved. The possible lines of communication are shown by the arrows in the diagram.[45]

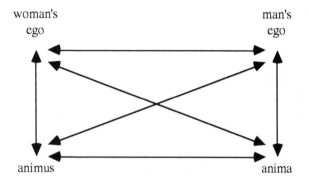

woman's ego   man's ego

animus   anima

While a man's task in assimilating the effects of the anima involves discovering his true feelings, a woman becomes familiar with the nature of the animus by constantly questioning her ideas and opinions.

> The technique of coming to terms with the animus is the same in principle as in the case of the anima; only here the woman must learn to criticize and hold her opinions at a distance; not in order to repress them, but, by investigating their origins, to penetrate more deeply into the background, where she will then discover the primordial images, just as the man does in his dealings with the anima.[46]

Anthropos. Original or primordial man, an archetypal image of wholeness in alchemy, religion and Gnostic philosophy.

> There is in the unconscious an already existing wholeness, the "homo totus" of the Western and the *Chên-yên* (true man) of

---

44 "Anima and Animus," CW 7, par. 334.
45 Adapted from "The Psychology of the Transference," CW 16, par. 422.
46 "Anima and Animus," CW 7, par. 336.

Chinese alchemy, the round primordial being who represents the greater man within, the Anthropos, who is akin to God.[47]

Apotropaic. Descriptive of "magical thinking," based on the desire to depotentiate the influence of an object or person.

Apotropaic actions are characteristic of introversion as a mode of psychological orientation.

> I have seen an introverted child who made his first attempts to walk only after he had learned the names of all the objects in the room he might touch.[48]

Apperception. A psychic process by which a new conscious content is articulated with similar, already existing contents in such a way that it is understood. (Compare **assimilation.**)

> Sense-perceptions tell us that something *is.* But they do not tell us *what* it is. This is told us not by the process of perception but by the process of *apperception,* and this has a highly complex structure. Not that sense-perception is anything simple; only, its complex nature is not so much psychic as physiological. The complexity of apperception, on the other hand, is psychic.[49]

Jung distinguishes *active* from *passive* apperception. In active apperception, the ego grabs hold of something new and comes to grips with it. In passive apperception, the new content forces itself upon consciousness, either from outside (through the senses) or from within (the unconscious). Apperception may also be either directed or undirected.

> In the former case we speak of "attention," in the latter case of "fantasy" or "dreaming." The directed processes are rational, the undirected irrational.[50]

Archaic. Primal or original. (See also **participation mystique.**)

---

[47] "The Personification of the Opposites," CW 14, par. 152.
[48] "Psychological Types," CW 6, par. 897.
[49] "The Structure of the Psyche," CW 8, par. 288.
[50] Ibid., par. 294.

Every civilized human being, however high his conscious development, is still an archaic man at the deeper levels of his psyche.[51]

In anthropology, the term archaic is generally descriptive of primitive psychology. Jung used it when referring to thoughts, fantasies
and feelings that are not consciously differentiated.

> Archaism attaches primarily to the fantasies of the unconscious, i.e.,
> to the products of unconscious fantasy activity which reach con-
> sciousness. An image has an archaic quality when it possesses un-
> mistakable mythological parallels. Archaic, too, are the associations-
> by-analogy of unconscious fantasy, and so is their symbolism. The
> relation of identity with an object, or *participation mystique,* is
> likewise archaic. Concretism of thought and feeling is archaic; also
> compulsion and inability to control oneself (ecstatic or trance state,
> possession, etc.). Fusion of the psychological functions, of thinking
> with feeling, feeling with sensation, feeling with intuition, and so
> on, is archaic, as is also the fusion of part of a function with its
> counterpart.[52]

Archetype. Primordial, structural elements of the human psyche.
(See also **archetypal image** and **instinct.**)

> Archetypes are systems of readiness for action, and at the same time
> images and emotions. They are inherited with the brain structure—
> indeed they are its psychic aspect. They represent, on the one hand, a
> very strong instinctive conservatism, while on the other hand they
> are the most effective means conceivable of instinctive adaptation.
> They are thus, essentially, the chthonic portion of the psyche . . .
> that portion through which the psyche is attached to nature.[53]

> It is not . . . a question of inherited *ideas* but of inherited *possibili-
> ties* of ideas. Nor are they individual acquisitions but, in the main,
> common to all, as can be seen from [their] universal occurrence.[54]

Archetypes are irrepresentable in themselves but their effects are
discernible in archetypal images and motifs.

---

51 "Archaic Man," CW 10, par. 105

52 "Definitions," CW 6, par. 684.

53 "Mind and Earth," CW 10, par. 53.

54 "Concerning the Archetypes and the Anima Concept," CW 9i, par. 136.

Archetypes . . . present themselves *as ideas and images,* like everything else that becomes a content of consciousness.[55]

Archetypes are, by definition, factors and motifs that arrange the psychic elements into certain images, characterized as archetypal, but in such a way that they can be recognized only from the effects they produce.[56]

Jung also described archetypes as "instinctual images," the forms which the instincts assume. He illustrated this using the simile of the spectrum.

The dynamism of instinct is lodged as it were in the infra-red part of the spectrum, whereas the instinctual image lies in the ultra-violet part. . . . The realization and assimilation of instinct never take place at the red end, i.e., by absorption into the instinctual sphere, but only through integration of the image which signifies and at the same time evokes the instinct, although in a form quite different from the one we meet on the biological level.[57]

INSTINCTS	ARCHETYPES
infrared ———————————————————— ultraviolet	
(Physiological: body symptoms, instinctual perceptions, etc.)	(Psychological: spirit, dreams, conceptions, images, fantasies, etc.)

Psychologically . . . the archetype as an image of instinct is a spiritual goal toward which the whole nature of man strives; it is the sea to which all rivers wend their way, the prize which the hero wrests from the fight with the dragon.[58]

Archetypes manifest both on a personal level, through complexes, and collectively, as characteristics of whole cultures. Jung believed it was the task of each age to understand anew their content and their effects.

---

[55] "On the Nature of the Psyche," CW 8, par. 435.
[56] "A Psychological Approach to the Trinity," CW 11, par. 222, note 2.
[57] "On the Nature of the Psyche," CW 8, par. 414.
[58] Ibid., par. 415.

We can never legitimately cut loose from our archetypal foundations unless we are prepared to pay the price of a neurosis, any more than we can rid ourselves of our body and its organs without committing suicide. If we cannot deny the archetypes or otherwise neutralize them, we are confronted, at every new stage in the differentiation of consciousness to which civilization attains, with the task of finding a new *interpretation* appropriate to this stage, in order to connect the life of the past that still exists in us with the life of the present, which threatens to slip away from it.[59]

Archetypal image. The form or representation of an **archetype** in consciousness. (See also **collective unconscious.**)

[The archetype is] a *dynamism* which makes itself felt in the numinosity and fascinating power of the archetypal image.[60]

Archetypal images, as universal patterns or motifs which come from the collective unconscious, are the basic content of religions, mythologies, legends and fairy tales.

An archetypal content expresses itself, first and foremost, in metaphors. If such a content should speak of the sun and identify with it the lion, the king, the hoard of gold guarded by the dragon, or the power that makes for the life and health of man, it is neither the one thing nor the other, but the unknown third thing that finds more or less adequate expression in all these similes, yet—to the perpetual vexation of the intellect—remains unknown and not to be fitted into a formula.[61]

On a personal level, archetypal motifs are patterns of thought or behavior that are common to humanity at all times and in all places.

For years I have been observing and investigating the products of the unconscious in the widest sense of the word, namely dreams, fantasies, visions, and delusions of the insane. I have not been able to avoid recognizing certain regularities, that is, *types.* There are types of *situations* and types of *figures* that repeat themselves frequently and have a corresponding meaning. I therefore employ the term

---

[59] "The Psychology of the Child Archetype," CW 9i, par. 267.
[60] "On the Nature of the Psyche," CW 8, par. 414.
[61] "The Psychology of the Child Archetype," CW 9i, par. 267

"motif" to designate these repetitions. Thus there are not only typical dreams but typical motifs in dreams. . . . [These] can be arranged under a series of archetypes, the chief of them being . . . the *shadow,* the *wise old man,* the *child* (including the child hero), the *mother* ("Primordial Mother" and "Earth Mother") as a supraordinate personality ("daemonic" because supraordinate), and her counterpart the *maiden,* and lastly the *anima* in man and the *animus* in woman.[62]

Assimilation. The process of integrating outer objects (persons, things, ideas, values) and unconscious contents into consciousness.

Assimilation is the approximation of a new content of consciousness to already constellated subjective material . . . . Fundamentally, [it] is a process of apperception, but is distinguished from apperception by this element of approximation to the subjective material. . . .

I use the term assimilation . . . as the approximation of object to subject in general, and with it I contrast *dissimilation,* as the approximation of subject to object, and a consequent alienation of the subject from himself in favour of the object, whether it be an external object or a "psychological" object, for instance an idea.[63]

Association. A spontaneous flow of interconnected thoughts and images around a specific idea, often determined by unconscious connections. (See also **Word Association Experiment.**)

Personal associations to images in dreams, together with amplification, are an important initial step in their interpretation.

Attitude. The readiness of the psyche to act or react in a certain way, based on an underlying psychological **orientation.** (See also **adaptation, type** and **typology.**)

From a great number of existing or possible attitudes I have singled out four; those, namely, that are primarily oriented by the four basic psychological functions: thinking, feeling, sensation, intuition. When any of these attitudes is *habitual,* thus setting a definite stamp on the character of an individual, I speak of a psychological type.

---

62 "The Psychological Aspects of the Kore," ibid., par. 309.
63 "Definitions," CW 6, pars. 685f.

These *function-types,* which one can call the thinking, feeling, sensation, and intuitive types, may be divided into two classes . . . the rational and the irrational. . . . A further division into two classes is permitted by the predominant trend of the movement of libido, namely introversion and extraversion.[64]

The whole psychology of an individual even in its most fundamental features is oriented in accordance with his habitual attitude. . . . [which is] a resultant of all the factors that exert a decisive influence on the psyche, such as innate disposition, environmental influences, experience of life, insights and convictions gained through differentiation, collective views, etc. . . .

At bottom, attitude is an individual phenomenon that eludes scientific investigation. In actual experience, however, certain typical attitudes can be distinguished . . . . When a function habitually predominates, a typical attitude is produced. . . . There is thus a typical thinking, feeling, sensation, and intuitive attitude.[65]

Adaptation to one's environment requires an appropriate attitude. But due to changing circumstances, no one attitude is permanently suitable. When a particular attitude is no longer appropriate, whether to internal or external reality, the stage is set for psychological difficulties (e.g., an outbreak of neurosis).

For example, a feeling-attitude that seeks to fulfil the demands of reality by means of empathy may easily encounter a situation that can only be solved through thinking. In this case the feeling-attitude breaks down and the progression of libido also ceases. The vital feeling that was present before disappears, and in its place the psychic value of certain conscious contents increases in an unpleasant way; subjective contents and reactions press to the fore and the situation becomes full of affect and ripe for explosions.[66]

The tension leads to conflict, the conflict leads to attempts at mutual repression, and if one of the opposing forces is successfully repressed a dissociation ensues, a splitting of the personality, or disunion with oneself.[67]

---

64 Ibid., par. 835.
65 Ibid., pars. 690f.
66 "On Psychic Energy," CW 8, par. 61.
67 Ibid.

Autonomous. Independent of the conscious will, associated in general with the nature of the unconscious and in particular with activated **complexes.**

Auxiliary function. A helpful second or third function, according to Jung's model of **typology,** that has a co-determining influence on consciousness.

> Absolute sovereignty always belongs, empirically, to one function alone, and *can* belong only to one function, because the equally independent intervention of another function would necessarily produce a different orientation which, partially at least, would contradict the first. But since it is a vital condition for the conscious process of adaptation always to have clear and unambiguous aims, the presence of a second function of equal power is naturally ruled out. This other function, therefore, can have only a secondary importance. . . . Its secondary importance is due to the fact that it is not, like the primary function . . . an absolutely reliable and decisive factor, but comes into play more as an auxiliary or complementary function.[68]

The auxiliary function is always one whose nature differs from, but is not antagonistic to, the superior or primary function: either of the irrational functions (intuition and sensation) can be auxiliary to one of the rational functions (thinking and feeling), and vice versa.

Thus thinking and intuition can readily pair, as can thinking and sensation, since the nature of intuition and sensation is not fundamentally opposed to the thinking function. Similarly, sensation can be bolstered by an auxiliary function of thinking or feeling, feeling is aided by sensation or intuition, and intuition goes well with feeling or thinking.

> The resulting combinations *[see figure opposite]* present the familiar picture of, for instance, practical thinking allied with sensation, speculative thinking forging ahead with intuition, artistic intuition selecting and presenting its images with the help of feeling-values, philosophical intuition systematizing its vision into comprehensive thought by means of a powerful intellect, and so on.[69]

---

[68] "General Description of the Types," CW 6, par. 667.
[69] Ibid., par. 669.

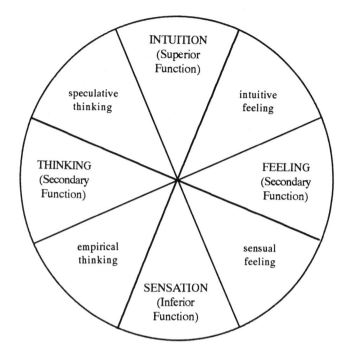

Axiom of Maria. A precept in alchemy: "One becomes two, two becomes three, and out of the third comes the one as the fourth."

Jung used the axiom of Maria as a metaphor for the whole process of individuation. *One* is the original state of unconscious wholeness; *two* signifies the conflict between opposites; *three* points to a potential resolution; *the third* is the transcendent function; and *the one as the fourth* is a transformed state of consciousness, relatively whole and at peace.

Cathartic method. A confessional approach to treating neurosis, involving the **abreaction** of emotions associated with a trauma.

> Through confession I throw myself into the arms of humanity again, freed at last from the burden of moral exile. The goal of the cathartic method is full confession—not merely the intellectual recognition of the facts with the head, but their confirmation by the heart and the actual release of suppressed emotion.[70]

---

[70] "Problems of Modern Psychotherapy," CW 16, par. 134.

Jung acknowledged the therapeutic value of catharsis, but early in his career he recognized its limitations in the process of analysis.

> The new psychology would have remained at the stage of confession had catharsis proved itself a panacea. First and foremost, however, it is not always possible to bring the patients close enough to the unconscious for them to perceive the shadows. . . . They have quite enough to confess already, they say; they do not have to turn to the unconscious for that.[71]

Causal. An approach to the interpretation of psychic phenomena based on cause and effect. (See also **final** and **reductive.**)

Child. Psychologically, an image of both the irrecoverable past and an anticipation of future development. (See also **incest.**)

> The "child" is . . . . both beginning and end, an initial and a terminal creature. . . . the pre-conscious and the post-conscious essence of man. His pre-conscious essence is the unconscious state of earliest childhood; his post-conscious essence is an anticipation by analogy of life after death. In this idea the all-embracing nature of psychic wholeness is expressed.[72]

Feelings of alienation or abandonment can constellate the child archetype. The effects are two-fold: the "poor-me" syndrome characteristic of the regressive longing for dependence, and, paradoxically, a desperate desire to be free of the past—the positive side of the divine child archetype.

> Abandonment, exposure, danger, etc., are all elaborations of the "child's" insignificant beginnings and of its mysterious and miraculous birth. This statement describes a certain psychic experience of a creative nature, whose object is the emergence of a new and as yet unknown content. In the psychology of the individual there is always, at such moments, an agonizing situation of conflict from which there seems to be no way out—at least for the conscious mind, since as far as this is concerned, *tertium non datur.*[73]

---

[71] Ibid., par. 137.

[72] "The Psychology of the Child Archetype," CW 9i, par. 299.

[73] Ibid., par. 285.

"Child" means something evolving towards independence. This it cannot do without detaching itself from its origins: abandonment is therefore a necessary condition [of consciousness], not just a con- comitant symptom.[74]

Circumambulation. A term used to describe the interpretation of an image by reflecting on it from different points of view.

Circumambulation differs from free association in that it is circu- lar, not linear. Where free association leads away from the original image, circumambulation stays close to it.

Collective. Psychic contents that belong not to one individual but to a society, a people or the human race in general. (See also **collec- tive unconscious, individuation** and **persona.**)

The conscious personality is a more or less arbitrary segment of the collective psyche. It consists in a sum of psychic factors that are felt to be personal.[75]

Identification with the collective and voluntary segregation from it are alike synonymous with disease.[76]

A collective quality adheres not only to particular psychic elements or contents but to whole psychological functions.

Thus the thinking function as a whole can have a collective quality, when it possesses general validity and accords with the laws of logic. Similarly, the feeling function as a whole can be collective, when it is identical with the general feeling and accords with general expecta- tions, the general moral consciousness, etc. In the same way, sensa- tion and intuition are collective when they are at the same time char- acteristic of a large group.[77]

Collective unconscious. A structural layer of the human psyche containing inherited elements, distinct from the **personal uncon- scious.** (See also **archetype** and **archetypal image.**)

---

[74] Ibid., par. 287.
[75] "The Persona as a Segment of the Collective Psyche," CW 7, par. 244.
[76] "The Structure of the Unconscious," ibid., par. 485
[77] "Definitions," CW 6, par. 692.

The collective unconscious contains the whole spiritual heritage of mankind's evolution, born anew in the brain structure of every individual.[78]

Jung derived his theory of the collective unconscious from the ubiquity of psychological phenomena that could not be explained on the basis of personal experience. Unconscious fantasy activity, for instance, falls into two categories.

First, fantasies (including dreams) of a personal character, which go back unquestionably to personal experiences, things forgotten or repressed, and can thus be completely explained by individual anamnesis. Second, fantasies (including dreams) of an impersonal character, which cannot be reduced to experiences in the individual's past, and thus cannot be explained as something individually acquired. These fantasy-images undoubtedly have their closest analogues in mythological types. . . . These cases are so numerous that we are obliged to assume the existence of a collective psychic substratum. I have called this the *collective unconscious.*[79]

The collective unconscious—so far as we can say anything about it at all—appears to consist of mythological motifs or primordial images, for which reason the myths of all nations are its real exponents. In fact, the whole of mythology could be taken as a sort of projection of the collective unconscious. . . . We can therefore study the collective unconscious in two ways, either in mythology or in the analysis of the individual.[80]

The more one becomes aware of the contents of the personal unconscious, the more is revealed of the rich layer of images and motifs that comprise the collective unconscious. This has the effect of enlarging the personality.

In this way there arises a consciousness which is no longer imprisoned in the petty, oversensitive, personal world of the ego, but participates freely in the wider world of objective interests. This widened consciousness is no longer that touchy, egotistical bundle of personal wishes, fears, hopes, and ambitions which always has to be

---

[78] "The Structure of the Psyche," CW 8, par. 342.

[79] "The Psychology of the Child Archetype," CW 9i, par. 262.

[80] "The Structure of the Psyche," CW 8, par. 325.

compensated or corrected by unconscious counter-tendencies; instead, it is a function of relationship to the world of objects, bringing the individual into absolute, binding, and indissoluble communion with the world at large.[81]

Compensation. A natural process aimed at establishing or maintaining balance within the psyche. (See also **active imagination, dreams, neurosis** and **self-regulation of the psyche.**)

> The activity of consciousness is *selective*. Selection demands *direction*. But direction requires the *exclusion of everything irrelevant.* This is bound to make the conscious orientation one-sided. The contents that are excluded and inhibited by the chosen direction sink into the unconscious, where they form a counterweight to the conscious orientation. The strengthening of this counterposition keeps pace with the increase of conscious one-sidedness until finally . . . . the repressed unconscious contents break through in the form of dreams and spontaneous images. . . . As a rule, the unconscious compensation does not run counter to consciousness, but is rather a balancing or supplementing of the conscious orientation. In dreams, for instance, the unconscious supplies all those contents that are constellated by the conscious situation but are inhibited by conscious selection, although a knowledge of them would be indispensable for complete adaptation.[82]

In neurosis, where consciousness is one-sided to an extreme, the aim of analytic therapy is the realization and assimilation of unconscious contents so that compensation may be reestablished. This can often be accomplished by paying close attention to dreams, emotions and behavior patterns, and through active imagination.

Complex. An emotionally charged group of ideas or images. (See also **Word Association Experiment.**)

> [A complex] is the *image* of a certain psychic situation which is strongly accentuated emotionally and is, moreover, incompatible with the habitual attitude of consciousness.[83]

---

[81] "The Function of the Unconscious," CW 7, par. 275.

[82] "Definitions," CW 6, par. 694.

[83] "A Review of the Complex Theory," CW 8, par. 201.

The *via regia* to the unconscious . . . is not the dream, as [Freud] thought, but the complex, which is the architect of dreams and of symptoms. Nor is this *via* so very "royal," either, since the way pointed out by the complex is more like a rough and uncommonly devious footpath.[84]

Formally, complexes are "feeling-toned ideas" that over the years accumulate around certain archetypes, for instance "mother" and "father." When complexes are constellated, they are invariably accompanied by affect. They are always relatively autonomous.

Complexes interfere with the intentions of the will and disturb the conscious performance; they produce disturbances of memory and blockages in the flow of associations; they appear and disappear according to their own laws; they can temporarily obsess consciousness, or influence speech and action in an unconscious way. In a word, complexes behave like independent beings.[85]

Complexes are in fact "splinter psyches." The aetiology of their origin is frequently a so-called trauma, an emotional shock or some such thing, that splits off a bit of the psyche. Certainly one of the commonest causes is a moral conflict, which ultimately derives from the apparent impossibility of affirming the whole of one's nature.[86]

Everyone knows nowadays that people "have complexes." What is not so well known, though far more important theoretically, is that complexes can *have us.*[87]

Jung stressed that complexes in themselves are not negative; only their effects often are. In the same way that atoms and molecules are the invisible components of physical objects, complexes are the building blocks of the psyche and the source of all human emotions.

Complexes are focal or nodal points of psychic life which we would not wish to do without; indeed, they should not be missing, for otherwise psychic activity would come to a fatal standstill.[88]

---

[84] Ibid., par. 210.

[85] "Psychological Factors in Human Behaviour," ibid., par. 253.

[86] "A Review of the Complex Theory," ibid., par. 204.

[87] Ibid., par. 200.

[88] "A Psychological Theory of Types," CW 6, par. 925.

Complexes obviously represent a kind of inferiority in the broadest sense . . . [but] to have complexes does not necessarily indicate inferiority. It only means that something discordant, unassimilated, and antagonistic exists, perhaps as an obstacle, but also as an incentive to greater effort, and so, perhaps, to new possibilities of achievement.[89]

Some degree of one-sidedness is unavoidable, and, in the same measure, complexes are unavoidable too.[90]

The negative effect of a complex is commonly experienced as a distortion in one or other of the psychological functions (feeling, thinking, intuition and sensation). In place of sound judgment and an appropriate feeling response, for instance, one reacts according to what the complex dictates. As long as one is unconscious of the complexes, one is liable to be driven by them.

The possession of complexes does not in itself signify neurosis . . . and the fact that they are painful is no proof of pathological disturbance. Suffering is not an illness; it is the normal counterpole to happiness. A complex becomes pathological only when we think we have not got it.[91]

Identification with a complex, particularly the anima/animus and the shadow, is a frequent source of neurosis. The aim of analysis in such cases is not to get rid of the complexes—as if that were possible—but to minimize their negative effects by understanding the part they play in behavior patterns and emotional reactions.

A complex can be really overcome only if it is lived out to the full. In other words, if we are to develop further we have to draw to us and drink down to the very dregs what, because of our complexes, we have held at a distance.[92]

Concretism. A way of thinking or feeling that is **archaic** and undifferentiated, based entirely on perception through sensation. (Compare **abstraction.**)

---

[89] Ibid., par. 925.

[90] "Psychological Factors in Human Behaviour," CW 8, par. 255.

[91] "Psychotherapy and a Philosophy of Life," CW 16, par. 179.

[92] "Psychological Aspects of the Mother Archetype," CW 9i, par. 184.

Concretism as a way of mental functioning is closely related to the more general concept of *participation mystique.* Concrete thinking and feeling are attuned to and bound by physiological stimuli and material facts. Such an orientation is valuable in the recognition of outer reality, but deficient in how it is interpreted.

> Concretism results in a projection of . . . inner factors into the objective data and produces an almost superstitious veneration of mere facts.[93]

> [Concrete thinking] has no detached independence but clings to material phenomena. It rises at most to the level of *analogy.* Primitive feeling is equally bound to material phenomena. Both of them depend on sensation and are only slight differentiated from it. Concretism, therefore, is an archaism. The magical influence of the fetish is not experienced as a subjective state of feeling, but sensed as a magical effect. That is concretistic feeling. The primitive does not experience the idea of the divinity as a subjective content; for him the sacred tree is the abode of the god, or even the god himself. That is concretistic thinking. In civilized man, concretistic thinking consists in the inability to conceive of anything except immediately obvious facts transmitted by the senses, or in the inability to discriminate between subjective feeling and the sensed object.[94]

Conflict. A state of indecision, accompanied by inner tension. (See also **opposites** and **transcendent function.**)

> The apparently unendurable conflict is proof of the rightness of your life. A life without inner contradiction is either only half a life or else a life in the Beyond, which is destined only for angels. But God loves human beings more than the angels.[95]

> The self is made manifest in the opposites and in the conflict between them; it is a *coincidentia oppositorum* [coincidence of opposites]. Hence the way to the self begins with conflict.[96]

---

[93] "Definitions," CW 6, par. 699.

[94] Ibid., par. 697.

[95] *C.G. Jung Letters,* vol. 1, p. 375.

[96] "Individual Dream Symbolism in Relation to Alchemy," CW 12, par. 259.

Conflict is a hallmark of neurosis, but conflict is not invariably neurotic. Some degree of conflict is even desirable since without some tension between opposites the developmental process is inhibited. Conflict only becomes neurotic when it interferes with the normal functioning of consciousness.

> The stirring up of conflict is a Luciferian virtue in the true sense of the word. Conflict engenders fire, the fire of affects and emotions, and like every other fire it has two aspects, that of combustion and that of creating light.[97]

When a conflict is unconscious, tension manifests as physical symptoms, particularly in the stomach, the back and the neck. Conscious conflict is experienced as moral or ethical tension. Serious conflicts, especially those involving love or duty, generally involve a disparity between the functions of thinking and feeling. If one or the other is not a conscious participant in the conflict, it needs to be introduced.

> The objection [may be] advanced that many conflicts are intrinsically insoluble. People sometimes take this view because they think only of external solutions—which at bottom are not solutions at all. . . . A real solution comes only from within, and then only because the patient has been brought to a different attitude.[98]

Jung's major contribution to the psychology of conflict was his belief that it had a purpose in terms of the self-regulation of the psyche. If the tension between the opposites can be held in consciousness, then something will happen internally to resolve the conflict. The solution, essentially irrational and unforeseeable, generally appears as a new attitude toward oneself and the outer situation, together with a sense of peace; energy previously locked up in indecision is released and the progression of libido becomes possible. Jung called this the *tertium non datur* or transcendent function, because what happens transcends the opposites.

Holding the tension between opposites requires patience and a strong ego, otherwise a decision will be made out of desperation.

---

[97] "Psychological Aspects of the Mother Archetype," CW 9i, par. 179.
[98] "Some Crucial Points in Psychoanalysis," CW 4, par. 606.

Then the opposite will be constellated even more strongly and the conflict will continue with renewed force.

Jung's basic hypothesis in working with neurotic conflict was that separate personalities in oneself—complexes—were involved. As long as these are not made conscious they are acted out externally, through projection. Conflicts with other people are thus essentially externalizations of an unconscious conflict within oneself.

Coniunctio. Literally, "conjunction," used in alchemy to refer to chemical combinations; psychologically, it points to the union of **opposites** and the birth of new possibilities.

> The *coniunctio* is an *a priori* image that occupies a prominent place in the history of man's mental development. If we trace this idea back we find it has two sources in alchemy, one Christian, the other pagan. The Christian source is unmistakably the doctrine of Christ and the Church, *sponsus* and *sponsa,* where Christ takes the role of Sol and the Church that of Luna. The pagan source is on the one hand the hieros-gamos, on the other the marital union of the mystic with God.[99]

Other alchemical terms used by Jung with a near-equivalent psychological meaning include *unio mystica* (mystic or sacred marriage), *coincidentia oppositorum* (coincidence of opposites), *complexio oppositorum* (the opposites embodied in a single image) *unus mundus* (one world) and Philosophers' Stone.

Consciousness. The function or activity which maintains the relation of psychic contents to the ego; distinguished conceptually from the **psyche,** which encompasses both consciousness and the unconscious. (See also **opposites.**)

> There is no consciousness without discrimination of opposites.[100]

> There are two distinct ways in which consciousness arises. The one is a moment of high emotional tension, comparable to the scene in *Parsifal* where the hero, at the very moment of greatest temptation, suddenly realizes the meaning of Amfortas' wound. The other is a

---

99 "The Psychology of the Transference," CW 16, par. 355.
100 "Psychological Aspects of the Mother Archetype," CW 9i, par. 178.

state of contemplation, in which ideas pass before the mind like dream-images. Suddenly there is a flash of association between two apparently disconnected and widely separated ideas, and this has the effect of releasing a latent tension. Such a moment often works like a revelation. In every case it seems to be the discharge of energy-tension, whether external or internal, which produces consciousness.[101]

In Jung's view of the psyche, individual consciousness is a superstructure based on, and arising out of, the unconscious.

Consciousness does not create itself—it wells up from unknown depths. In childhood it awakens gradually, and all through life it wakes each morning out of the depths of sleep from an unconscious condition. It is like a child that is born daily out of the primordial womb of the unconscious. . . . It is not only influenced by the unconscious but continually emerges out of it in the form of numberless spontaneous ideas and sudden flashes of thought.[102]

Constellate. To activate, usually used with reference to a **complex** and an accompanying pattern of emotional reactions.

This term simply expresses the fact that the outward situation releases a psychic process in which certain contents gather together and prepare for action. When we say that a person is "constellated" we mean that he has taken up a position from which he can be expected to react in a quite definite way. . . . The constellated contents are definite complexes possessing their own specific energy.[103]

Constructive. An approach to the interpretation of psychic activity based on its goal or purpose rather than its cause or source. (See also **final**; compare **reductive**.)

I use *constructive* and *synthetic* to designate a method that is the antithesis of reductive. The constructive method is concerned with the elaboration of the products of the unconscious (dreams, fantasies, etc.). It takes the unconscious product as a symbolic expression which anticipates a coming phase of psychological development.[104]

---

101 "Analytical Psychology and Education," CW 17, par. 207.
102 "The Psychology of Eastern Meditation," CW 11, par. 935.
103 "A Review of the Complex Theory," CW 8, par. 198.
104 "Definitions," CW 6, par. 701.

The constructive or synthetic method of treatment presupposes insights which are at least potentially present in the patient and can therefore be made conscious.[105]

The constructive method involves both the amplification of symbols and their interpretation on the subjective level. Its use in dream interpretation aims at understanding how the conscious orientation may be modified in light of the dream's symbolic message. This is in line with Jung's belief that the psyche is a self-regulating system.

In the treatment of neurosis, Jung saw the constructive method as complementary, not in opposition, to the reductive approach of classical psychoanalysis.

> We apply a largely reductive point of view in all cases where it is a question of illusions, fictions, and exaggerated attitudes. On the other hand, a constructive point of view must be considered for all cases where the conscious attitude is more or less normal, but capable of greater development and refinement, or where unconscious tendencies, also capable of development, are being misunderstood and kept under by the conscious mind.[106]

Countertransference. A particular case of **projection,** used to describe the unconscious emotional response of the analyst to the analysand in a therapeutic relationship. (See also **transference.**)

> A transference is answered by a counter-transference from the analyst when it projects a content of which he is unconscious but which nevertheless exists in him. The counter-transference is then just as useful and meaningful, or as much of a hindrance, as the transference of the patient, according to whether or not it seeks to establish that better rapport which is essential for the realization of certain unconscious contents. Like the transference, the counter-transference is compulsive, a forcible tie, because it creates a "mystical" or unconscious identity with the object.[107]

A workable analytic relationship is predicated on the assumption that the analyst is not as neurotic as the analysand. Although a

---

[105] "The Transcendent Function," CW 8, par. 145.

[106] "Analytical Psychology and Education," CW 17, par. 195.

[107] "General Aspects of Dream Psychology," CW 8, par. 519.

lengthy personal analysis is the major requirement in the training of analysts, this is no guarantee against projection.

> Even if the analyst has no neurosis, but only a rather more extensive area of unconsciousness than usual, this is sufficient to produce a sphere of mutual unconsciousness, i.e., a counter-transference. This phenomenon is one of the chief occupational hazards of psychotherapy. It causes psychic infections in both analyst and patient and brings the therapeutic process to a standstill. This state of unconscious identity is also the reason why an analyst can help his patient just so far as he himself has gone and not a step further.[108]

Crucifixion. An archetypal motif associated with **conflict** and the problem of the **opposites.**

> Nobody who finds himself on the road to wholeness can escape that characteristic suspension which is the meaning of crucifixion. For he will infallibly run into things that thwart and "cross" him: first, the thing he has no wish to be (the shadow); second, the thing he is not (the "other," the individual reality of the "You"); and third, his psychic non-ego (the collective unconscious).[109]

Depotentiate. The process of removing energy from an unconscious content by assimilating its meaning.

Depression. A psychological state characterized by lack of energy. (See also **abaissement du niveau mental, final, libido, night sea journey** and **regression.**)
Energy not available to consciousness does not simply vanish. It regresses and stirs up unconscious contents (fantasies, memories, wishes, etc.) that for the sake of psychological health need to be brought to light and examined.

> Depression should therefore be regarded as an unconscious compensation whose content must be made conscious if it is to be fully effective. This can only be done by consciously regressing along with the depressive tendency and integrating the memories so activated into

---

[108] "Appendix," CW 16, par. 545.
[109] "The Psychology of the Transference," ibid., par. 470.

the conscious mind—which was what the depression was aiming at in the first place.[110]

Depression is not necessarily pathological. It often foreshadows a renewal of the personality or a burst of creative activity.

There are moments in human life when a new page is turned. New interests and tendencies appear which have hitherto received no attention, or there is a sudden change of personality (a so-called mutation of character). During the incubation period of such a change we can often observe a loss of conscious energy: the new development has drawn off the energy it needs from consciousness. This lowering of energy can be seen most clearly before the onset of certain psychoses and also in the empty stillness which precedes creative work.[111]

Differentiation. The separation of parts from a whole, necessary for conscious access to the psychological **functions.**

So long as a function is still so fused with one or more other functions—thinking with feeling, feeling with sensation, etc.—that it is unable to operate on its own, it is in an *archaic* condition, i.e., not differentiated, not separated from the whole as a special part and existing by itself. Undifferentiated thinking is incapable of thinking apart from other functions; it is continually mixed up with sensations, feelings, intuitions, just as undifferentiated feeling is mixed up with sensations and fantasies.[112]

An undifferentiated function is characterized by ambivalence (every position entails its own negative), which leads to characteristic inhibitions in its use.

Differentiation consists in the separation of the function from other functions, and in the separation of its individual parts from each other. Without differentiation direction is impossible, since the direction of a function towards a goal depends on the elimination of anything irrelevant. Fusion with the irrelevant precludes direction; only a differentiated function is *capable* of being directed.[113]

---

110 "The Sacrifice," CW 5, par. 625.
111 "The Psychology of the Transference," CW 16, par. 373.
112 "Definitions," CW 6, par. 705.
113 Ibid., par. 705.

Dissociation. The **splitting** of a personality into its component parts or **complexes,** characteristic of **neurosis.**

> A dissociation is not healed by being split off, but by more complete disintegration. All the powers that strive for unity, all healthy desire for selfhood, will resist the disintegration, and in this way he will become conscious of the possibility of an inner integration, which before he had always sought outside himself. He will then find his reward in an undivided self.[114]

In the analysis of neurotic breakdowns, the aim is to make the conscious ego aware of autonomous complexes. This can be done both through reductive analysis and by objectifying them in the process of active imagination.

> Every form of communication with the split-off part of the psyche is therapeutically effective. This effect is also brought about by the real or merely supposed discovery of the causes. Even when the discovery is no more than an assumption or a fantasy, it has a healing effect at least by suggestion if the analyst himself believes in it and makes a serious attempt to understand.[115]

Dreams. Independent, spontaneous manifestations of the unconscious; fragments of involuntary psychic activity just conscious enough to be reproducible in the waking state.

> Dreams are neither deliberate nor arbitrary fabrications; they are natural phenomena which are nothing other than what they pretend to be. They do not deceive, they do not lie, they do not distort or disguise. . . . They are invariably seeking to express something that the ego does not know and does not understand.[116]

In symbolic form, dreams picture the current situation in the psyche from the point of view of the unconscious.

> Since the meaning of most dreams is *not* in accord with the tendencies of the conscious mind but shows peculiar deviations, we must assume that the unconscious, the matrix of dreams, has an indepen-

---

114 "Marriage as a Psychological Relationship," CW 17, pars. 334f.
115 "The Philosophical Tree," CW 13, par. 465.
116 "Analytical Psychology and Education," CW 17, par. 189.

dent function. This is what I call the autonomy of the unconscious. The dream not only fails to obey our will but very often stands in flagrant opposition to our conscious intentions.[117]

Jung acknowledged that in some cases dreams have a wish-fulfilling and sleep-preserving function (Freud) or reveal an infantile striving for power (Adler), but he focused on their symbolic content and their compensatory role in the self-regulation of the psyche: they reveal aspects of oneself that are not normally conscious, they disclose unconscious motivations operating in relationships and present new points of view in conflict situations.

> In this regard there are three possibilities. If the conscious attitude to the life situation is in large degree one-sided, then the dream takes the opposite side. If the conscious has a position fairly near the "middle," the dream is satisfied with variations. If the conscious attitude is "correct" (adequate), then the dream coincides with and emphasizes this tendency, though without forfeiting its peculiar autonomy.[118]

In Jung's view, a dream is an interior drama.

> The whole dream-work is essentially subjective, and a dream is a theatre in which the dreamer is himself the scene, the player, the prompter, the producer, the author, the public, and the critic.[119]

This conception gives rise to the interpretation of dreams on the subjective level, where the images in them are seen as symbolic representations of elements in the dreamer's own personality. Interpretation on the objective level refers the images to people and situations in the outside world.

Many dreams have a classic dramatic structure. There is an *exposition* (place, time and characters), which shows the initial situation of the dreamer. In the second phase there is a *development* in the plot (action takes place). The third phase brings the culmination or *climax* (a decisive event occurs). The final phase is the *lysis,* the result or solution (if any) of the action in the dream.

---

[117] "On the Nature of Dreams," CW 8, par. 545.

[118] Ibid., par. 546.

[119] "General Aspects of Dream Psychology," ibid., par. 509.

Ego. The central complex in the field of **consciousness**. (See also **self.**)

> The ego, the subject of consciousness, comes into existence as a complex quantity which is constituted partly by the inherited disposition (character constituents) and partly by unconsciously acquired impressions and their attendant phenomena.[120]

Jung pointed out that knowledge of the ego-personality is often confused with self-understanding.

> Anyone who has any ego-consciousness at all takes it for granted that he knows himself. But the ego knows only its own contents, not the unconscious and its contents. People measure their self-knowledge by what the average person in their social environment knows of himself, but not by the real psychic facts which are for the most part hidden from them. In this respect the psyche behaves like the body, of whose physiological and anatomical structure the average person knows very little too.[121]

In the process of individuation, one of the initial tasks is to differentiate the ego from the complexes in the personal unconscious, particularly the persona, the shadow and anima/animus. A strong ego can relate objectively to these and other contents of the unconscious without identifying with them. Because the ego experiences itself as the center of the psyche, it is especially difficult to resist identification with the self, to which it owes its existence and to which, in the hierarchy of the psyche, it is subordinate.

> The ego stands to the self as the moved to the mover, or as object to subject, because the determining factors which radiate out from the self surround the ego on all sides and are therefore supraordinate to it. The self, like the unconscious, is an *a priori* existent out of which the ego evolves.[122]

Identification with the self can manifest in two ways: the *assimilation of the ego by the self,* in which case the ego falls under the control of the unconscious; or the *assimilation of the self to the ego,*

---

[120] "Analytical Psychology and Education," CW 17, par. 169.
[121] "The Undiscovered Self," CW 10, par. 491.
[122] "Transformation Symbolism in the Mass," CW 11, par. 391.

where the ego becomes overaccentuated. In both cases the result is inflation, with disturbances in adaptation.

> In the first case, reality has to be protected against an archaic . . . dream-state; in the second, room must be made for the dream at the expense of the world of consciousness. In the first case, mobilization of all the virtues is indicated; in the second, the presumption of the ego can only be damped down by moral defeat.[123]

Emotion. An involuntary reaction due to an active **complex.** (See also **affect.**)

> On the one hand, emotion is the alchemical fire whose warmth brings everything into existence and whose heat burns all superfluities to ashes *(omnes superfluitates comburit)*. But on the other hand, emotion is the moment when steel meets flint and a spark is struck forth, for emotion is the chief source of consciousness. There is no change from darkness to light or from inertia to movement without emotion.[124]

Empathy. An introjection of the object, based on the unconscious **projection** of subjective contents. (Compare **identification.**)

> Empathy presupposes a subjective attitude of confidence, or trustfulness towards the object. It is a readiness to meet the object halfway, a subjective assimilation that brings about a good understanding between subject and object, or at least simulates it.[125]

In contrast to abstraction, associated with introversion, empathy corresponds to the attitude of extraversion.

> The man with the empathetic attitude finds himself . . . in a world that needs his subjective feeling to give it life and soul. He animates it with himself.[126]

Enantiodromia. Literally, "running counter to," referring to the emergence of the unconscious **opposite** in the course of time.

---

123 "The Self," CW 9ii, par. 47.
124 "Psychological Aspects of the Mother Archetype," CW 9i, par. 179.
125 "The Type Problem in Aesthetics," CW 6, par. 489.
126 Ibid., par. 492.

This characteristic phenomenon practically always occurs when an extreme, one-sided tendency dominates conscious life; in time an equally powerful counterposition is built up, which first inhibits the conscious performance and subsequently breaks through the conscious control.[127]

Enantiodromia is typically experienced in conjunction with symptoms associated with acute neurosis, and often foreshadows a rebirth of the personality.

The grand plan on which the unconscious life of the psyche is constructed is so inaccessible to our understanding that we can never know what evil may not be necessary in order to produce good by enantiodromia, and what good may very possibly lead to evil.[128]

Energic. See final.

Eros. In Greek mythology, the personification of love, a cosmogonic force of nature; psychologically, the function of relationship. (See also **anima, animus, Logos** and **mother complex**.)

Woman's consciousness is characterized more by the connective quality of Eros than by the discrimination and cognition associated with Logos. In men, Eros . . . is usually less developed than Logos. In women, on the other hand, Eros is an expression of their true nature, while their Logos is often only a regrettable accident.[129]

Eros is a questionable fellow and will always remain so . . . . He belongs on one side to man's primordial animal nature which will endure as long as man has an animal body. On the other side he is related to the highest forms of the spirit. But he thrives only when spirit and instinct are in right harmony.[130]

Where love reigns, there is no will to power; and where the will to power is paramount, love is lacking. The one is but the shadow of the other: the man who adopts the standpoint of Eros finds his com-

---

127 "Definitions," ibid., par. 709.
128 "The Phenomenology of the Spirit in Fairytales," CW 9i, par. 397.
129 "The Syzygy: Anima and Animus," CW 9ii, par. 29.
130 "The Eros Theory," CW 7, par. 32.

pensatory opposite in the will to power, and that of the man who puts the accent on power is Eros.[131]

An unconscious Eros always expresses itself as will to power.[132]

Extraversion. A mode of psychological **orientation** where the movement of energy is toward the outer world. (Compare **introversion.**)

> Extraversion is characterized by interest in the external object, responsiveness, and a ready acceptance of external happenings, a desire to influence and be influenced by events, a need to join in and get "with it," the capacity to endure bustle and noise of every kind, and actually find them enjoyable, constant attention to the surrounding world, the cultivation of friends and acquaintances, none too carefully selected, and finally by the great importance attached to the figure one cuts.[133]

Jung believed that introversion and extraversion were present in everyone, but that one attitude-type is invariably dominant. When external factors are the prime motivating force for judgments, perceptions, affects and actions, we have an extraverted attitude or type.

> The extravert's philosophy of life and his ethics are as a rule of a highly collective nature with a strong streak of altruism, and his conscience is in large measure dependent on public opinion.[134]

Jung believed that type differentiation begins very early in life, so that it might be described as innate.

> The earliest sign of extraversion in a child is his quick adaptation to the environment, and the extraordinary attention he gives to objects and especially to the effect he has on them. Fear of objects is minimal; he lives and moves among them with confidence. . . . and can therefore play with them freely and learn through them. He likes to carry his enterprises to the extreme and exposes himself to risks. Everything unknown is alluring.[135]

---

[131] "The Problem of the Attitude-Type," ibid., par. 78.
[132] "Psychological Aspects of the Mother Archetype," CW 9i, par. 167.
[133] "Psychological Typology," CW 6, par. 972.
[134] Ibid.
[135] "Psychological Types," ibid., par. 896.

In general, the extravert trusts what is received from the outside world and is not inclined to examine personal motivations.

> He has no secrets he has not long since shared with others. Should something unmentionable nevertheless befall him, he prefers to forget it. Anything that might tarnish the parade of optimism and positivism is avoided. Whatever he thinks, intends, and does is displayed with conviction and warmth.[136]

Although everyone is affected by objective data, the extravert's thoughts, decisions and behavior are determined by them. Personal views and the inner life take second place to outer conditions.

> He lives in and through others; all self-communings give him the creeps. Dangers lurk there which are better drowned out by noise. If he should ever have a "complex," he finds refuge in the social whirl and allows himself to be assured several times a day that everything is in order.[137]

The psychic life of the extreme extraverted type is enacted wholly in reaction to the environment, which determines the personal standpoint. If the mores change, he adjusts his views and behavior patterns to match. This is both a strength and a limitation.

> Adjustment is not adaptation; adaptation . . . requires observance of laws more universal than the immediate conditions of time and place. The very adjustment of the normal extraverted type is his limitation. He owes his normality . . . to his ability to fit into existing conditions with comparative ease. His requirements are limited to the objectively possible, for instance to the career that holds out good prospects at this particular moment; he does what is needed of him, or what is expected of him, and refrains from all innovations that are not entirely self-evident or that in any way exceed the expectations of those around him.[138]

Extraversion is an asset in social situations and in relating to the external environment. But a too-extraverted attitude may result in sacrificing oneself in order to fulfil what one sees as objective de-

---

[136] "Psychological Typology," ibid., par. 973.
[137] Ibid., par. 974.
[138] "General Description of the Types," CW 6, par. 564.

mands—the needs of others, for instance, or the requirements of an expanding business.

> This is the extravert's danger: He gets sucked into objects and completely loses himself in them. The resultant functional disorders, nervous or physical, have a compensatory value, as they force him into an involuntary self-restraint. Should the symptoms be functional, their peculiar character may express his psychological situation in symbolic form; for instance, a singer whose fame has risen to dangerous heights that tempt him to expend too much energy suddenly finds he cannot sing high notes . . . . Or a man of modest beginnings who rapidly reaches a social position of great influence with wide prospects is suddenly afflicted with all the symptoms of mountain sickness.[139]

The form of neurosis most likely to afflict the extravert is hysteria, which typically manifests as a pronounced identification with persons in the immediate environment.

The extravert's tendency to sacrifice inner reality to outer circumstances is not a problem as long as the extraversion is not too extreme. But to the extent that it becomes necessary to compensate the inclination to one-sidedness, there will arise a markedly self-centered tendency in the unconscious. All those needs or desires that are stifled or repressed by the conscious attitude come in the back door, in the form of infantile thoughts and emotions that center on oneself.

> The more complete the conscious attitude of extraversion is, the more infantile and archaic the unconscious attitude will be. The egoism which characterizes the extravert's unconscious attitude goes far beyond mere childish selfishness; it verges on the ruthless and brutal.[140]

The danger then is that the extravert, so habitually and apparently selflessly attuned to the outside world and the needs of others, may suddenly become quite indifferent.

Fantasy. A complex of ideas or imaginative activity expressing the flow of psychic energy. (See also **active imagination**.)

---

[139] Ibid., par. 565.
[140] Ibid., par. 572.

A fantasy needs to be understood both causally and purposively. Causally interpreted, it seems like a *symptom* of a physiological state, the outcome of antecedent events. Purposively interpreted, it seems like a *symbol,* seeking to characterize a definite goal with the help of the material at hand, or trace out a line of future psychological development.[141]

Jung distinguished between *active* and *passive* fantasies. The former, characteristic of the creative mentality, are evoked by an intuitive attitude directed toward the perception of unconscious contents; passive fantasies are spontaneous and autonomous manifestations of unconscious complexes.

Passive fantasy, therefore, is always in need of conscious *criticism,* lest it merely reinforce the standpoint of the unconscious opposite. Whereas active fantasy, as the product of a conscious attitude *not* opposed to the unconscious, and of unconscious processes not opposed but merely compensatory to consciousness, does not require criticism so much as *understanding.*[142]

Jung developed the method of active imagination as a way of assimilating the meaning of fantasies. The important thing is not to interpret but to experience them.

Continual conscious realization of unconscious fantasies, together with active participation in the fantastic events, has . . . the effect firstly of extending the conscious horizon by the inclusion of numerous unconscious contents; secondly of gradually diminishing the dominant influence of the unconscious; and thirdly of bringing about a change of personality.[143]

Father complex. A group of feeling-toned ideas associated with the experience and image of father. (See also **Logos.**)

In men, a positive father-complex very often produces a certain credulity with regard to authority and a distinct willingness to bow down before all spiritual dogmas and values; while in women, it induces the liveliest spiritual aspirations and interests. In dreams, it is

---

[141] "Definitions," CW 6, par. 720.

[142] Ibid., par. 714.

[143] "The Technique of Differentiation," CW 7, par. 358.

always the father-figure from whom the decisive convictions, prohibitions, and wise counsels emanate.[144]

Jung's comments on the father complex were rarely more than asides in writing about something else. In general, the father complex in a man manifests in the persona (through identification) and as aspects of his shadow; in a woman, it manifests in the nature of the animus, colored by the projection of her father's anima.

> The father exerts his influence on the mind or spirit of his daughter—on her "Logos." This he does by increasing her intellectuality, often to a pathological degree which in my later writings I have described as "animus possession."[145]

> The father is the first carrier of the animus-image. He endows this virtual image with substance and form, for on account of his Logos he is the source of "spirit" for the daughter. Unfortunately this source is often sullied just where we would expect clean water. For the spirit that benefits a woman is not mere intellect, it is far more: it is an attitude, the spirit by which a man lives. Even a so-called "ideal" spirit is not always the best if it does not understand how to deal adequately with nature, that is, with animal man. . . . Hence every father is given the opportunity to corrupt, in one way or another, his daughter's nature, and the educator, husband, or psychiatrist then has to face the music. For "what has been spoiled by the father"[146] can only be made good by a father.[147]

Feeling. The psychological **function** that evaluates or judges what something or someone is worth. (Compare **thinking.**)

> A feeling is as indisputable a reality as the existence of an idea.[148]

The feeling function is the basis for "fight or flight" decisions. As a subjective process, it may be quite independent of external stimuli. In Jung's view it is a rational function, like thinking, in that it is de-

---

[144] "The Phenomenology of the Spirit in Fairytales," CW 9i, par. 396.

[145] "The Origin of the Hero," CW 5, par. 272.

[146] A reference to Hexagram 18 in the *I Ching* (Richard Wilhelm edition, p. 80): "Work on What Has Been Spoiled."

[147] "The Personification of the Opposites," CW 14, par. 232.

[148] "The Psychology of the Transference," CW 16, par. 531.

cisively influenced not by perception (as are the functions of sensation and intuition) but by reflection. A person whose overall attitude is oriented by the feeling function is called a feeling type.

In everyday usage, feeling is often confused with emotion. The latter, more appropriately called affect, is the result of an activated complex. Feeling not contaminated by affect can be quite cold.

> Feeling is distinguished from affect by the fact that it produces no perceptible physical innervations, i.e., neither more nor less than an ordinary thinking process.[149]

Feminine. See **anima, Eros** and **Logos.**

Final. A point of view based on the potential result or purpose of psychic activity, complementary to a causal approach. (See also **constructive, neurosis, reductive,** and **self-regulation of the psyche.**)

> Psychological data necessitate a twofold point of view, namely that of *causality* and that of *finality*. I use the word finality intentionally, in order to avoid confusion with the concept of teleology.[150] By finality I mean merely the immanent psychological striving for a goal. Instead of "striving for a goal" one could also say "sense of purpose." All psychological phenomena have some such sense of purpose inherent in them, even merely reactive phenomena like emotional reactions.[151]

Jung also called the final point of view energic, contrasting it with mechanistic or reductive.

> The mechanistic view is purely causal; it conceives an event as the effect of a cause, in the sense that unchanging substances change their relations to one another according to fixed laws. The energic point of view on the other hand is in essence final; the event is traced back from effect to cause on the assumption that some kind of energy underlies the changes in phenomena, that it maintains itself

---

[149] "Definitions," CW 6, par. 725.

[150] Teleology implies the anticipation of a particular end or goal; finality assumes purpose but an essentially unknown goal.

[151] "General Aspects of Dream Psychology," CW 8, par. 456.

as a constant throughout these changes and finally leads to entropy, a condition of general equilibrium. The flow of energy has a definite direction (goal) in that it follows the gradient of potential in a way that cannot be reversed.[152]

Jung believed that laws governing the physical conservation of energy applied equally to the psyche. Psychologically, this means that where there is an overabundance of energy in one place, some other psychic function has been deprived; conversely, when libido "disappears," as it seems to do in a depression, it must appear in another form, for instance as a symptom.

> Every time we come across a person who has a "bee in his bonnet," or a morbid conviction, or some extreme attitude, we know that there is too much libido, and that the excess must have been taken from somewhere else where, consequently, there is too little. . . . Thus the symptoms of a neurosis must be regarded as exaggerated functions over-invested with libido. . . .
>
> The question has to be reversed in the case of those syndromes characterized mainly by lack of libido, for instance apathetic states. Here we have to ask, where did the libido go? . . . The libido is there, but it is not visible and is inaccessible to the patient himself. . . . It is the task of psychoanalysis to search out that hidden place where the libido dwells.[153]

The energic or final point of view, coupled with the concept of compensation, led Jung to believe that an outbreak of neurosis is essentially an attempt by the psyche to cure itself.

Fourth function. See **inferior function.**

Function. A form of psychic activity, or manifestation of libido, that remains the same in principle under varying conditions. (See also **auxiliary function, differentiation, inferior function, primary function** and **typology.**)

Jung's model of typology distinguishes four psychological functions: thinking, feeling, sensation and intuition.

---

152 "On Psychic Energy," ibid., pars. 2f.
153 "The Theory of Psychoanalysis," CW 4, pars. 254f.

Sensation establishes what is actually present, thinking enables us to recognize its meaning, feeling tells us its value, and intuition points to possibilities as to whence it came and whither it is going in a given situation.[154]

Though all the functions exist in every psyche, one function is invariably more consciously developed than the others, giving rise to a one-sidedness that often leads to neurosis.

The more [a man] identifies with one function, the more he invests it with libido, and the more he withdraws libido from the other functions. They can tolerate being deprived of libido for even quite long periods, but in the end they will react. Being drained of libido, they gradually sink below the threshold of consciousness, lose their associative connection with it, and finally lapse into the unconscious. This is a regressive development, a reversion to the infantile and finally to the archaic level. . . . [which] brings about a dissociation of the personality.[155]

Hero. An archetypal motif based on overcoming obstacles and achieving certain goals.

The hero's main feat is to overcome the monster of darkness: it is the long-hoped-for and expected triumph of consciousness over the unconscious.[156]

The hero myth is an unconscious drama seen only in projection, like the happenings in Plato's parable of the cave.[157]

The hero symbolizes a man's *unconscious self,* and this manifests itself empirically as the sum total of all archetypes and therefore includes the archetype of the father and of the wise old man. To that extent the hero is his own father and his own begetter.[158]

Mythologically, the hero's goal is to find the treasure, the princess, the ring, the golden egg, elixir of life, etc. Psychologically these are metaphors for one's true feelings and unique potential. In

---

[154] "A Psychological Theory of Types," CW 6, par. 958.

[155] "The Type Problem in Aesthetics," ibid., pars. 502f.

[156] "The Psychology of the Child Archetype," CW 9i, par. 284.

[157] "The Dual Mother," CW 5, par. 612.

[158] Ibid., par. 516.

the process of individuation, the heroic task is to assimilate unconscious contents as opposed to being overwhelmed by them. The potential result is the release of energy that has been tied up with unconscious complexes.

> In myths the hero is the one who conquers the dragon, not the one who is devoured by it. And yet both have to deal with the same dragon. Also, he is no hero who never met the dragon, or who, if he once saw it, declared afterwards that he saw nothing. Equally, only one who has risked the fight with the dragon and is not overcome by it wins the hoard, the "treasure hard to attain." He alone has a genuine claim to self-confidence, for he has faced the dark ground of his self and thereby has gained himself. . . . He has acquired the right to believe that he will be able to overcome all future threats by the same means.[159]

The hero's journey is a round, as illustrated in the diagram.[160]

CALL TO ADVENTURE

---

[159] "The Conjunction," CW 14, par. 756.
[160] Adapted from Joseph Campbell, *Hero with a Thousand Faces,* Bollingen Series XVII (Princeton: Princeton University Press, 1949), p. 245.

In myth and legend, the hero typically travels by ship, fights a sea monster, is swallowed, struggles against being bitten or crushed to death, and having arrived inside the belly of the whale, like Jonah, seeks the vital organ and cuts it off, thereby winning release. Eventually he must return to his beginnings and bear witness.

In terms of a man's individuation, the whale-dragon is the mother or the mother-bound anima. The vital organ that must be severed is the umbilical cord.

> The hero is the ideal masculine type: leaving the mother, the source of life, behind him, he is driven by an unconscious desire to find her again, to return to her womb. Every obstacle that rises in his path and hampers his ascent wears the shadowy features of the Terrible Mother, who saps his strength with the poison of secret doubt and retrospective longing.[161]

In a woman's psychology, the hero's journey is lived out through the worldly exploits of the animus, or else in a male partner, through projection.

Homosexuality. Usually characterized psychologically by identification with the **anima.** (See also **mother complex.**)

Jung acknowledged the potential neurotic effects of homosexuality, but he did not see it as an illness in itself.

> In view of the recognized frequency of this phenomenon, its interpretation as a pathological perversion is very dubious. The psychological findings show that it is rather a matter of incomplete detachment from the hermaphroditic archetype, coupled with a distinct resistance to identify with the role of a one-sided sexual being. Such a disposition should not be adjudged negative in all circumstances, in so far as it preserves the archetype of the Original Man, which a one-sided sexual being has, up to a point, lost.[162]

Hostile brothers. An archetypal motif associated with the opposites constellated in a **conflict** situation.

---

[161] "The Dual Mother," CW 5, par. 611.
[162] "Concerning the Archetypes and the Anima Concept," CW 9i, par. 146.

Examples of the hostile brothers motif in mythology are the struggle between Gilgamesh and Enkidu in *The Gilgamesh Epic,* and the Biblical story of Cain and Abel. Psychologically, it is generally interpreted in terms of the tug of war between ego and shadow.

Hysteria. A state of mind marked by an exaggerated rapport with persons in the immediate environment and an adjustment to surrounding conditions that amounts to imitation.

> Hysteria is, in my view, by far the most frequent neurosis of the extraverted type. . . . A constant tendency to make himself interesting and produce an impression is a basic feature of the hysteric. The corollary of this is his proverbial suggestibility, his proneness to another person's influence. Another unmistakable sign of the extraverted hysteric is his effusiveness, which occasionally carries him into the realm of fantasy, so that he is accused of the "hysterical lie."[163]

Hysterical neurosis is usually accompanied by compensatory reactions from the unconscious.

> [These] counteract the exaggerated extraversion by means of physical symptoms that force the libido to introvert. The reaction of the unconscious produces another class of symptoms having a more introverted character, one of the most typical being a morbid intensification of fantasy activity.[164]

Identification. A psychological process in which the personality is partially or totally dissimilated. (See also **participation mystique** and **projection.**)

Identity, denoting an unconscious conformity between subject and object, oneself and others, is the basis for identification, projection and introjection.

> Identity is responsible for the naïve assumption that the psychology of one man is like that of another, that the same motives occur everywhere, that what is agreeable to me must obviously be pleasurable for others, that what I find immoral must also be immoral for

---

[163] "General Description of the Types," CW 6, par. 566.
[164] Ibid., par. 566.

them, and so on. It is also responsible for the almost universal desire to correct in others what most needs correcting in oneself.[165]

Identification facilitates early adaptation to the outside world, but in later life becomes a hindrance to individual development.

For example, identification with the father means, in practice, adopting all the father's ways of behaving, as though the son were the same as the father and not a separate individuality. Identification differs from *imitation* in that it is an *unconscious* imitation, whereas imitation is a conscious copying. . . . Identification can be beneficial so long as the individual cannot go his own way. But when a better possibility presents itself, identification shows its morbid character by becoming just as great a hindrance as it was an unconscious help and support before. It now has a dissociative effect, splitting the individual into two mutually estranged personalities.[166]

Identification with a complex (experienced as possession) is a frequent source of neurosis, but it is also possible to identify with a particular idea or belief.

The ego keeps its integrity only if it does not identify with one of the opposites, and if it understands how to hold the balance between them. This is possible only if it remains conscious of both at once. However, the necessary insight is made exceedingly difficult not by one's social and political leaders alone, but also by one's religious mentors. They all want decision in favour of one thing, and therefore the utter identification of the individual with a necessarily one-sided "truth." Even if it were a question of some great truth, identification with it would still be a catastrophe, as it arrests all further spiritual development.[167]

One-sidedness is usually due to identifying with a particular conscious attitude. This can result in losing touch with the compensating powers of the unconscious.

In a case like this the unconscious usually responds with violent emotions, irritability, lack of control, arrogance, feelings of inferiority, moods, depressions, outbursts of rage, etc., coupled with lack of

---

[165] "Definitions," ibid., par. 742.
[166] Ibid., par. 738.
[167] "On the Nature of the Psyche," CW 8, par. 425.

self-criticism and the misjudgments, mistakes, and delusions which this entails.[168]

Image, primordial. See **archetype** and **archetypal image.**

Imago. A term used to differentiate the objective reality of a person or a thing from the subjective perception of its importance.

The image we form of a human object is, to a very large extent, subjectively conditioned. In practical psychology, therefore, we would do well to make a rigorous distinction between the image or *imago* of a man and his real existence. Because of its extremely subjective origin, the *imago* is frequently more an image of a subjective functional complex than of the object itself. In the analytical treatment of unconscious products it is essential that the *imago* should not be assumed to be identical with the object; it is better to regard it as an image of the subjective relation to the object.[169]

Imagos are the consequence of personal experience combined with archetypal images in the collective unconscious. Like everything else unconscious, they are experienced in projection.

The more limited a man's field of consciousness is, the more numerous the psychic contents (imagos) which meet him as quasi-external apparitions, either in the form of spirits, or as magical potencies projected upon living people (magicians, witches, etc.)[170]

Incest. Psychologically, the regressive longing for the security of childhood and early youth.

Jung interpreted incest images in dreams and fantasies not concretely but symbolically, as indicating the need for a new adaptation more in accord with the instincts. (This differed so radically from the psychoanalytic view that it led to his break with Freud.)

So long as the child is in that state of unconscious identity with the mother, he is still one with the animal psyche and is just as unconscious as it. The development of consciousness inevitably leads not

---

[168] "The Philosophical Tree," CW 13, par. 454.
[169] "Definitions," CW 6, par. 812.
[170] "The Function of the Unconscious," CW 7, par. 295.

only to separation from the mother, but to separation from the parents and the whole family circle and thus to a relative degree of detachment from the unconscious and the world of instinct. Yet the longing for this lost world continues and, when difficult adaptations are demanded, is forever tempting one to make evasions and retreats, to regress to the infantile past, which then starts throwing up the incestuous symbolism.[171]

Whenever [the] drive for wholeness appears, it begins by disguising itself under the symbolism of incest, for, unless he seeks it in himself, a man's nearest feminine counterpart is to be found in his mother, sister, or daughter.[172]

Individual. Unique and unlike anyone else, distinguished from what is **collective.** (See also **individuality.**)

A distinction must be made between *individuality* and the *individual.* The individual is determined on the one hand by the principle of uniqueness and distinctiveness, and on the other by the society to which he belongs. He is an indispensable link in the social structure.[173]

The individual is precisely that which can never be merged with the collective and is never identical with it.[174]

The larger a community is, and the more the sum total of collective factors peculiar to every large community rests on conservative prejudices detrimental to individuality, the more will the individual be morally and spiritually crushed, and, as a result, the one source of moral and spiritual progress for society is choked up.[175]

The individual standpoint is not antagonistic to collective norms, only differently oriented.

The individual way can never be directly opposed to the collective norm, because the opposite of the collective norm could only be an-

---

171 "Symbols of the Mother and of Rebirth," CW 5, par. 351.
172 "The Psychology of the Transference," CW 16, par. 471.
173 "The Structure of the Unconscious," CW 7, par. 519.
174 Ibid., par. 485.
175 "The Assimilation of the Unconscious," ibid., par. 240.

other, but contrary, norm. But the individual way can, by definition, never be a norm.[176]

Jung believed that the survival of the individual within a group depended not only on psychological self-understanding, but also on the personal experience of a higher truth.

The individual will never find the real justification for his existence and his own spiritual and moral autonomy anywhere except in an extramundane principle capable of relativizing the overpowering influence of external factors. . . . For this he needs the evidence of inner, transcendent experience which alone can protect him from the otherwise inevitable submersion in the mass.[177]

Resistance to the organized mass can be effected only by the man who is as well organized in his individuality as the mass itself.[178]

Individualism. A belief in the supremacy of individual interests over those of the collective, not to be confused with **individuality** or **individuation.**

Individualism means deliberately stressing and giving prominence to some supposed peculiarity rather than to collective considerations and obligations. But individuation means precisely the better and more complete fulfilment of the collective qualities of the human being, since adequate consideration of the peculiarity of the individual is more conducive to a better social performance than when the peculiarity is neglected or suppressed.

. . . . Since the universal factors always appear only in individual form, a full consideration of them will also produce an individual effect, and one which cannot be surpassed by anything else, least of all by individualism.[179]

Individuality. The qualities or characteristics that distinguish one person from another. (See also **personality.**)

By individuality I mean the peculiarity and singularity of the individual in every psychological respect. Everything that is not *collec-*

---

176 "Definitions," CW 6, par. 761.

177 "The Undiscovered Self," CW 10, par. 511.

178 Ibid., par. 540 (italics in original).

179 "The Function of the Unconscious," CW 7, pars. 267f.

tive is individual, everything in fact that pertains only to one individual and not to a larger group of individuals.[180]

The psychological individual, or his individuality, has an *a priori* unconscious existence, but exists consciously only so far as a consciousness of his peculiar nature is present . . . . A conscious process of differentiation, or individuation, is needed to bring the individuality to consciousness, i.e., to raise it out of the state of identity with the object.[181]

In the undifferentiated psyche, individuality is subjectively identified with the persona but is actually possessed by an inner, unrecognized aspect of oneself. In such cases, one's individuality is commonly experienced in another person, through projection. If and when this situation becomes intolerable to the psyche, appropriate images appear in an attempt at compensation.

This . . . frequently gives rise in dreams to the symbol of psychic pregnancy, a symbol that goes back to the primordial image of the hero's birth. The child that is to be born signifies the individuality, which, though present, is not yet conscious.[182]

Individuation. A process of psychological **differentiation,** having for its goal the development of the **individual** personality.

In general, it is the process by which individual beings are formed and differentiated; in particular, it is the development of the psychological individual as a being distinct from the general, collective psychology.[183]

The aim of individuation is nothing less than to divest the self of the false wrappings of the persona on the one hand, and of the suggestive power of primordial images on the other.[184]

Individuation is a process informed by the archetypal ideal of wholeness, which in turn depends on a vital relationship between

---

180 "Definitions," CW 6, par. 756.
181 Ibid., par. 755.
182 Ibid., par. 806.
183 Ibid., par. 757.
184 "The Function of the Unconscious," CW 7, par. 269.

ego and unconscious. The aim is not to overcome one's personal psychology, to become perfect, but to become familiar with it. Thus individuation involves an increasing awareness of one's unique psychological reality, including personal strengths and limitations, and at the same time a deeper appreciation of humanity in general.

As the individual is not just a single, separate being, but by his very existence presupposes a collective relationship, it follows that the process of individuation must lead to more intense and broader collective relationships and not to isolation.[185]

Individuation does not shut one out from the world, but gathers the world to itself.[186]

Individuation has two principle aspects: in the first place it is an internal and subjective process of integration, and in the second it is an equally indispensable process of objective relationship. Neither can exist without the other, although sometimes the one and sometimes the other predominates.[187]

Individuation and a life lived by collective values are nevertheless two divergent destinies. In Jung's view they are related to one another by guilt. Whoever embarks on the personal path becomes to some extent estranged from collective values, but does not thereby lose those aspects of the psyche which are inherently collective. To atone for this "desertion," the individual is obliged to create something of worth for the benefit of society.

Individuation cuts one off from personal conformity and hence from collectivity. That is the guilt which the individuant leaves behind him for the world, that is the guilt he must endeavor to redeem. He must offer a ransom in place of himself, that is, he must bring forth values which are an equivalent substitute for his absence in the collective personal sphere. Without this production of values, final individuation is immoral and—more than that—suicidal. . . .

The individuant has no *a priori* claim to any kind of esteem. He has to be content with whatever esteem flows to him from outside by virtue of the values he creates. Not only has society a right, it

---

185 "Definitions," CW 6, par. 758.
186 "On the Nature of the Psyche," CW 8, par. 432.
187 "The Psychology of Transference," CW 16, par. 448.

also has a duty to condemn the individuant if he fails to create equivalent values.[188]

Individuation differs from individualism in that the former deviates from collective norms but retains respect for them, while the latter eschews them entirely.

> A real conflict with the collective norm arises only when an individual way is raised to a norm, which is the actual aim of extreme individualism. Naturally this aim is pathological and inimical to life. It has, accordingly, nothing to do with individuation, which, though it may strike out on an individual bypath, precisely on that account needs the norm for its orientation to society and for the vitally necessary relationship of the individual to society. Individuation, therefore, leads to a natural esteem for the collective norm.[189]

The process of individuation, consciously pursued, leads to the realization of the self as a psychic reality greater than the ego. Thus individuation is essentially different from the process of simply becoming conscious.

> The goal of the individuation process is the synthesis of the self.[190]

> Again and again I note that the individuation process is confused with the coming of the ego into consciousness and that the ego is in consequence identified with the self, which naturally produces a hopeless conceptual muddle. Individuation is then nothing but ego-centredness and autoeroticism. But the self comprises infinitely more than a mere ego, as the symbolism has shown from of old. It is as much one's self, and all other selves, as the ego.[191]

In Jung's view, no one is ever completely individuated. While the goal is wholeness and a healthy working relationship with the self, the true value of individuation lies in what happens along the way.

> The goal is important only as an idea; the essential thing is the *opus* which leads to the goal: *that* is the goal of a lifetime.[192]

---

[188] "Adaptation, Individuation, Collectivity," CW 18, pars. 1095f.
[189] "Definitions," CW 6, par. 761.
[190] "The Psychology of the Child Archetype," CW 9i, par. 278.
[191] "On the Nature of the Psyche," CW 8, par. 432.
[192] "The Psychology of the Transference," CW 16, par. 400.

Inferior function. The least differentiated of the four psychological functions. (Compare **primary function.**)

> The inferior function is practically identical with the dark side of the human personality.[193]

In Jung's model of typology, the inferior or fourth function is opposite to the superior or primary function. Whether it operates in an introverted or extraverted way, it behaves like an autonomous complex; its activation is marked by affect and it resists integration.

> The inferior function secretly and mischievously influences the superior function most of all, just as the latter represses the former most strongly.[194]

> Positive as well as negative occurrences can constellate the inferior counter-function. When this happens, sensitiveness appears. Sensitiveness is a sure sign of of the presence of inferiority. This provides the psychological basis for discord and misunderstanding, not only as between two people, but also in ourselves. The essence of the inferior function is autonomy: it is independent, it attacks, it fascinates and so spins us about that we are no longer masters of ourselves and can no longer rightly distinguish between ourselves and others.[195]

The inferior function is always of the same nature, rational or irrational, as the primary function: when thinking is most developed, the other rational function, feeling, is inferior; if sensation is dominant, then intuition, the other irrational function, is the fourth function, and so on. This accords with general experience: the thinker is tripped up by feeling values; the practical sensation type gets into a rut, blind to the possibilities seen by intuition; the feeling type is deaf to logical thinking; and the intuitive, at home in the inner world, runs afoul of concrete reality.

One may be aware of the perceptions or judgments associated with the inferior function, but these are generally over-ridden by the superior function. Thinking types, for example, do not give their feelings much weight. Sensation types have intuitions, but they are not moti-

---

193 "Concerning Rebirth," CW 9i, par. 222.
194 "The Phenomenology of the Spirit in Fairytales," ibid., par. 431.
195 "The Problem of the Attitude-Type," CW 7, par. 85.

vated by them. Similarly, feeling types brush away disturbing thoughts and intuitives ignore what is right in front of them.

Although the inferior function may be conscious as a phenomenon its true significance nevertheless remains unrecognized. It behaves like many repressed or insufficiently appreciated contents, which are partly conscious and partly unconscious . . . . Thus in normal cases the inferior function remains conscious, at least in its effects; but in a neurosis it sinks wholly or in part into the unconscious. [196]

To the extent that a person functions too one-sidedly, the inferior function becomes correspondingly primitive and troublesome. The overly dominant primary function takes energy away from the inferior function, which falls into the unconscious. There it is prone to be activated in an unnatural way, giving rise to infantile desires and other symptoms of imbalance. This is the situation in neurosis.

In order to extricate the inferior function from the unconscious by analysis, the unconscious fantasy formations that have now been activated must be brought to the surface. The conscious realization of these fantasies brings the inferior function to consciousness and makes further development possible. [197]

When it becomes desirable or necessary to develop the inferior function, this can only happen gradually.

I have frequently observed how an analyst, confronted with a terrific thinking type, for instance, will do his utmost to develop the feeling function directly out of the unconscious. Such an attempt is foredoomed to failure, because it involves too great a violation of the conscious standpoint. Should the violation nevertheless be successful, a really compulsive dependence of the patient on the analyst ensues, a transference that can only be brutally terminated, because, having been left without a standpoint, the patient has made his standpoint the analyst. . . . [Therefore] in order to cushion the impact of the unconscious, an irrational type needs a stronger development of the rational auxiliary function present in consciousness [and vice versa]. [198]

---

[196] "Definitions," CW 6, par. 764.
[197] Ibid., par. 764.
[198] "General Description of the Types," ibid., par. 670.

Attempts to assimilate the inferior function are usually accompanied by a deterioration in the primary function. The thinking type can't write an essay, the sensation type gets lost and forgets appointments, the intuitive loses touch with possibilities, and the feeling type can't decide what something's worth.

> And yet it is necessary for the development of character that we should allow the other side, the inferior function, to find expression. We cannot in the long run allow one part of our personality to be cared for symbiotically by another; for the moment when we might have need of the other function may come at any time and find us unprepared.[199]

Inflation. A state of mind characterized by an exaggerated sense of self-importance, often compensated by feelings of inferiority. (See also **mana-personality** and **negative inflation.**)

Inflation, whether positive or negative, is a symptom of psychological possession, indicating the need to assimilate unconscious complexes or disidentify from the self.

> An inflated consciousness is always egocentric and conscious of nothing but its own existence. It is incapable of learning from the past, incapable of understanding contemporary events, and incapable of drawing right conclusions about the future. It is hypnotized by itself and therefore cannot be argued with. It inevitably dooms itself to calamities that must strike it dead. Paradoxically enough, inflation is a regression of consciousness into unconsciousness. This always happens when consciousness takes too many unconscious contents upon itself and loses the faculty of discrimination, the *sine qua non* of all consciousness.[200]

> [Inflation] should not be interpreted as . . . conscious self-aggrandizement. Such is far from being the rule. In general we are not directly conscious of this condition at all, but can at best infer its existence indirectly from the symptoms. These include the reactions of our immediate environment. Inflation magnifies the blind spot in the eye.[201]

---

[199] "The Problem of the Attitude-Type," CW 7, par. 86.
[200] "Epilogue," CW 12, par. 563.
[201] "The Self," CW 9ii, par. 44.

Instinct. An involuntary drive toward certain activities. (See also **archetype** and **archetypal image**.)

All psychic processes whose energies are not under conscious control are instinctive.[202]

Instincts in their original strength can render social adaptation almost impossible.[203]

Instinct is not an isolated thing, nor can it be isolated in practice. It always brings in its train archetypal contents of a spiritual nature, which are at once its foundation and its limitation. In other words, an instinct is always and inevitably coupled with something like a philosophy of life, however archaic, unclear, and hazy this may be. Instinct stimulates thought, and if a man does not think of his own free will, then you get compulsive thinking, for the two poles of the psyche, the physiological and the mental, are indissolubly connected.[204]

Psychic processes which ordinarily are consciously controlled can become instinctive when imbued with unconscious energy. This is liable to occur when the level of consciousness is low, due to fatigue, intoxication, depression, etc. Conversely, instincts can be modified according to the extent that they are civilized and under conscious control, a process Jung called psychization.

An instinct which has undergone too much psychization can take its revenge in the form of an autonomous complex. This is one of the chief causes of neurosis.[205]

Too much of the animal distorts the civilized man, too much civilization makes sick animals.[206]

Jung identified five prominent groups of instinctive factors: creativity, reflection, activity, sexuality and hunger.

Hunger is a primary instinct of self-preservation, perhaps the most fundamental of all drives. *Sexuality* is a close second, particularly

---

[202] "Definitions," CW 6, par. 765.
[203] "The Transcendent Function," CW 8, par. 161.
[204] "Psychotherapy and a Philosophy of Life," CW 16, par. 185.
[205] "Psychological Factors in Human Behaviour," CW 8, par. 255.
[206] "The Eros Theory," CW 7, par. 32.

prone to psychization, which makes it possible to divert its purely biological energy into other channels. The urge to *activity* manifests in travel, love of change, restlessness and play. Under *reflection,* Jung included the religious urge and the search for meaning.

Creativity was for Jung in a class by itself. His descriptions of it refer specifically to the impulse to create art.

> Though we cannot classify it with a high degree of accuracy, the *creative instinct* is something that deserves special mention. I do not know if "instinct" is the correct word. We use the term "creative instinct" because this factor behaves at least dynamically, like an instinct. Like instinct it is compulsive, but it is not common, and it is not a fixed and invariably inherited organization. Therefore I prefer to designate the creative impulse as a psychic factor similar in nature to instinct, having indeed a very close connection with the instincts, but without being identical with any one of them. Its connections with sexuality are a much discussed problem and, furthermore, it has much in common with the drive to activity and the reflective instinct. But it can also suppress them, or make them serve it to the point of the self-destruction of the individual. Creation is as much destruction as construction.[207]

Jung also believed that true creativity could only be enhanced by the analytic process.

> Creative power is mightier than its possessor. If it is not so, then it is a feeble thing, and given favourable conditions will nourish an endearing talent, but no more. If, on the other hand, it is a neurosis, it often takes only a word or a look for the illusion to go up in smoke. . . . Disease has never yet fostered creative work; on the contrary, it is the most formidable obstacle to creation. No breaking down of repressions can ever destroy true creativeness, just as no analysis can ever exhaust the unconscious.[208]

Instinct and archetype are a pair of opposites, inextricably linked and therefore often difficult to tell apart.

> Psychic processes seem to be balances of energy flowing between spirit and instinct, though the question of whether a process is to be

---

[207] "Psychological Factors in Human Behaviour," CW 8, par. 245.
[208] "Analytical Psychology and Education," CW 17, par. 206.

described as spiritual or as instinctual remains shrouded in darkness. Such evaluation or interpretation depends entirely upon the standpoint or state of the conscious mind.[209]

When consciousness become overspiritualized, straying too far from its instinctual foundation, self-regulating processes within the psyche become active in an attempt to correct the balance. This is often signaled in dreams by animal symbols, particularly snakes.

> The snake is the representative of the world of instinct, especially of those vital processes which are psychologically the least accessible of all. Snake dreams always indicate a discrepancy between the attitude of the conscious mind and instinct, the snake being a personification of the threatening aspect of that conflict.[210]

Introjection. A process of **assimilation** of object to subject, the opposite of **projection.**

> Introjection is a process of extraversion, since assimilation to the object requires empathy and an investment of the object with libido. A *passive* and an *active* introjection may be distinguished: transference phenomena in the treatment of the neuroses belong to the former category, and, in general, all cases where the object exercises a compelling influence on the subject, while empathy as a process of adaptation belongs to the latter category.[211]

Introspection. A process of **reflection** that focuses on personal reactions, behavior patterns and attitudes. (See also **meditation.**)

The difference between introspection and introversion is that the latter refers to the direction in which energy naturally moves, while the former refers to self-examination. Neither introverts nor those with a well-developed thinking function have a monopoly on introspection.

Introversion. A mode of psychological **orientation** where the movement of energy is toward the inner world. (Compare **extraversion.**)

---

[209] "On the Nature of the Psyche," CW 8, par. 407.
[210] "The Sacrifice," CW 5, par. 615.
[211] "Definitions," CW 6, par. 768.

Everyone whose attitude is introverted thinks, feels, and acts in a way that clearly demonstrates that the subject is the prime motivating factor and that the object is of secondary importance.[212]

Always he has to prove that everything he does rests on his own decisions and convictions, and never because he is influenced by anyone, or desires to please or conciliate some person or opinion.[213]

An introverted consciousness can be well aware of external conditions, but is not motivated by them. The extreme introvert responds primarily to internal impressions.

In a large gathering he feels lonely and lost. The more crowded it is, the greater becomes his resistance. He is not in the least "with it," and has no love of enthusiastic get-togethers. He is not a good mixer. What he does, he does in his own way, barricading himself against influences from outside. . . . Under normal conditions he is pessimistic and worried, because the world and human beings are not in the least good but crush him. . . .

His own world is a safe harbour, a carefully tended and walled-in garden, closed to the public and hidden from prying eyes. His own company is the best.[214]

Signs of introversion in a child are a reflective, thoughtful manner and resistance to outside influences.

The child wants his own way, and under no circumstances will he submit to an alien rule he cannot understand. When he asks questions, it is not from curiosity or a desire to create a sensation, but because he wants names, meanings, explanations to give him subjective protection against the object.[215]

The introverted attitude tends to devalue things and other persons, to deny their importance. Hence, by way of compensation, extreme introversion leads to an unconscious reinforcement of the object's influence. This makes itself felt as a tie, with concomitant emotional reactions, to outer circumstances or another person.

---

212 Ibid., par. 769.
213 "Psychological Types," CW 6, par. 893.
214 "Psychological Typology," ibid., pars. 976f.
215 "Psychological Types," ibid., par. 897.

The individual's freedom of mind is fettered by the ignominy of his financial dependence, his freedom of action trembles in the face of public opinion, his moral superiority collapses in a morass of inferior relationships, and his desire to dominate ends in a pitiful craving to be loved. It is now the unconscious that takes care of the relation to the object, and it does so in a way that is calculated to bring the illusion of power and the fantasy of superiority to utter ruin.[216]

A person in this situation can be worn out from fruitless attempts to impose his or her will.

These efforts are constantly being frustrated by the overwhelming impressions received from the object. It continually imposes itself on him against his will, it arouses in him the most disagreeable and intractable affects and persecutes him at every step. A tremendous inner struggle is needed all the time in order to "keep going." The typical form his neurosis takes is psychasthenia, a malady characterized on the one hand by extreme sensitivity and on the other by great proneness to exhaustion and chronic fatigue.[217]

In less extreme cases, introverts are simply more conservative than not, preferring the familiar surroundings of home and intimate times with a few close friends; they husband their energy and would rather stay put than go from place to place. Their best work is done on their own resources, on their own initiative and in their own way.

His retreat into himself is not a final renunciation of the world, but a search for quietude, where alone it is possible for him to make his contribution to the life of the community.[218]

Intuition. The psychic function that perceives possibilities inherent in the present. (Compare **sensation.**)

Intuition gives outlook and insight; it revels in the garden of magical possibilities as if they were real.[219]

In Jung's model of typology, intuition, like sensation, is an irrational function because its apprehension of the world is based on the

---

[216] "General Description of the Types," ibid., par. 626.
[217] Ibid.
[218] "Psychological Typology," ibid., par. 979.
[219] "The Psychology of the Transference," CW 16, par. 492.

perception of given facts. Unlike sensation, however, it perceives via the unconscious and is not dependent on concrete reality.

> In intuition a content presents itself whole and complete, without our being able to explain or discover how this content came into existence. Intuition is a kind of instinctive apprehension, no matter of what contents. . . . Intuitive knowledge possesses an intrinsic certainty and conviction.[220]

Intuition may receive information from within (for instance, as a flash of insight of unknown origin), or be stimulated by what is going on in someone else.

> The first is a perception of unconscious psychic data originating in the subject, the second is a perception of data dependent on subliminal perceptions of the object and on the feelings and thoughts they evoke.[221]

Irrational. Not grounded in reason. (Compare **rational.**)

Jung pointed out that elementary existential facts fall into this category—for instance, that the earth has a moon, that chlorine is an element or that water freezes at a certain temperature and reaches its greatest density at four degrees centigrade—as does chance. They are irrational not because they are illogical, but because they are *beyond* reason.

In Jung's model of typology, the psychological functions of intuition and sensation are described as irrational.

> Both intuition and sensation are functions that find fulfilment in the *absolute perception* of the flux of events. Hence, by their very nature, they will react to every possible occurrence and be attuned to the absolutely contingent, and must therefore lack all rational direction. For this reason I call them irrational functions, as opposed to thinking and feeling, which find fulfilment only when they are in complete harmony with the laws of reason.[222]

> Merely because [irrational types] subordinate judgment to perception, it would be quite wrong to regard them as "unreasonable." It would

---

[220] "Definitions," CW 6, par. 770.
[221] Ibid., par. 771.
[222] Ibid., pars. 776f.

be truer to say that they are in the highest degree *empirical.* They base themselves entirely on experience.[223]

Kore. In Greek mythology, a term for the personification of feminine innocence (e.g., Persephone); psychologically, in man or woman, it refers to an archetypal image of potential renewal.

The phenomenology of the Kore is essentially bipolar (as is that of any archetype), associated with the mother-maiden dyad. When observed in the products of a woman's unconscious, it is an image of the supraordinate personality or self. In a man, the Kore is an aspect of the anima and partakes in all the symbolism attached to his inner personality.

As a matter of practical observation, the Kore often appears in woman as an *unknown young girl* . . . . The maiden's helplessness exposes her to all sorts of *dangers,* for instance of being devoured by reptiles or ritually slaughtered like a beast of sacrifice. Often there are bloody, cruel, and even obscene *orgies* to which the innocent child falls victim. Sometimes it is a true *nekyia,* a descent into Hades and a quest for the "treasure hard to attain," occasionally connected with orgiastic sexual rites or offerings of menstrual blood to the moon. Oddly enough, the various tortures and obscenities are carried out by an "Earth Mother." . . . The maiden who crops up in case histories differs not inconsiderably from the vaguely flower-like Kore in that the modern figure is more sharply delineated and not nearly so "unconscious."[224]

Demeter and Kore, mother and daughter, extend the feminine consciousness both upwards and downwards. They add an "older and younger," "stronger and weaker" dimension to it and widen out the narrowly limited conscious mind bound in space and time, giving it intimations of a greater and more comprehensive personality which has a share in the eternal course of things. . . . We could therefore say that every mother contains her daughter in herself and every daughter her mother, and that every woman extends backwards into her mother and forwards into her daughter. . . . The conscious experience of these ties produces the feeling that her life is spread out over generations—the first step towards the immediate experience

---

[223] "General Description of the Types," ibid., par. 616.
[224] "The Psychological Aspects of the Kore," CW 9i, par. 311.

and conviction of being outside time, which brings with it a feeling of *immortality.*[225]

Libido. Psychic energy in general. (See also **final.**)

Libido can never be apprehended except in a definite form; that is to say, it is identical with fantasy-images. And we can only release it from the grip of the unconscious by bringing up the corresponding fantasy-images.[226]

Jung specifically distanced his concept of libido from that of Freud, for whom it had a predominantly sexual meaning.

All psychological phenomena can be considered as manifestations of energy, in the same way that all physical phenomena have been understood as energic manifestations ever since Robert Mayer discovered the law of the conservation of energy. Subjectively and psychologically, this energy is conceived as *desire.* I call it *libido,* using the word in its original sense, which is by no means only sexual.[227]

[Libido] denotes a desire or impulse which is unchecked by any kind of authority, moral or otherwise. Libido is appetite in its natural state. From the genetic point of view it is bodily needs like hunger, thirst, sleep, and sex, and emotional states or affects, which constitute the essence of libido.[228]

In line with his belief that the psyche is a self-regulating system, Jung associated libido with intentionality. It "knows" where it ought to go for the overall health of the psyche.

The libido has, as it were, a natural penchant: it is like water, which must have a gradient if it is to flow.[229]

Where there is a lack of libido (depression), it has backed up (regressed) in order to stir up unconscious contents, the aim being to compensate the attitudes of consciousness. What little energy is left resists being applied in a consciously chosen direction.

---

225 Ibid., par. 316.
226 "The Technique of Differentiation," CW 7, par. 345.
227 "Psychoanalysis and Neurosis," CW 4, par. 567.
228 "The Concept of Libido," CW 5, par. 194.
229 "Symbols of the Mother and of Rebirth," ibid., par. 337.

It does not lie in our power to transfer "disposable" energy at will to a rationally chosen object. The same is true in general of the apparently disposable energy which is disengaged when we have destroyed its unserviceable forms through the corrosive of reductive analysis. [It] can at best be applied voluntarily for only a short time. But in most cases it refuses to seize hold, for any length of time, of the possibilities rationally presented to it. Psychic energy is a very fastidious thing which insists on fulfilment of its own conditions. However much energy may be present, we cannot make it serviceable until we have succeeded in finding the right gradient.[230]

The analytic task in such a situation is to discover the natural gradient of the person's energy.

What is it, at this moment and in this individual, that represents the natural urge of life? That is the question.[231]

Logos. The principle of logic and structure, traditionally associated with spirit, the father world and the God-image. (See also **animus** and **Eros.**)

There is no consciousness without discrimination of opposites. This is the paternal principle, the Logos, which eternally struggles to extricate itself from the primal warmth and primal darkness of the maternal womb; in a word, from unconsciousness.[232]

In Jung's earlier writings, he intuitively equated masculine consciousness with the concept of Logos and feminine consciousness with that of Eros. Either one could be dominant in a particular man or woman, due to the contrasexual complexes.

By Logos I meant discrimination, judgment, insight, and by Eros I meant the capacity to relate. I regarded both concepts as intuitive ideas which cannot be defined accurately or exhaustively. From the scientific point of view this is regrettable, but from a practical one it has its value, since the two concepts mark out a field of experience which it is equally difficult to define.

As we can hardly ever make a psychological proposition without

---

230 "The Problem of the Attitude-Type," CW 7, par. 76.
231 "The Structure of the Unconscious," ibid., par. 488.
232 "Psychological Aspects of the Mother Archetype," CW 9i, par. 178.

immediately having to reverse it, instances to the contrary leap to the eye at once: men who care nothing for discrimination, judgment, and insight, and women who display an almost excessively masculine proficiency in this respect. . . . Wherever this exists, we find a forcible intrusion of the unconscious, a corresponding exclusion of the consciousness specific to either sex, predominance of the shadow and of contrasexuality.[233]

In his later writing on alchemy, Jung described Logos and Eros as psychologically equivalent to solar and lunar consciousness, archetypal ideas analogous to the Eastern concepts of *yang* and *yin*—different qualities of energy. This did not change his view that Eros was more "specific" to feminine consciousness and Logos to masculine. Hence he attributed Eros in a man to the influence of the anima, and Logos in a woman to that of the animus.

In a man it is the lunar anima, in a woman the solar animus, that influences consciousness in the highest degree. Even if a man is often unaware of his own anima-possession, he has, understandably enough, all the more vivid an impression of the animus-possession of his wife, and vice versa.[234]

Loss of soul. A concept borrowed from anthropology, referring psychologically to a state of general malaise.

The peculiar condition covered by this term is accounted for in the mind of the primitive by the supposition that a soul has gone off, just like a dog that runs away from his master overnight. It is then the task of the medicine man to fetch the fugitive back. . . . Something similar can happen to civilized man, only he does not describe it as "loss of soul" but as an "abaissement du niveau mental."[235]

Mana-personality. A personified archetypal image of a supernatural force.

The mana-personality is a dominant of the collective unconscious, the well-known archetype of the mighty man in the form of hero,

---

[233] "The Personification of the Opposites," CW 14, pars. 224f.
[234] Ibid., par. 225.
[235] "Concerning Rebirth," CW 9i, par. 213.

chief, magician, medicine-man, saint, the ruler of men and spirits, the friend of God.[236]

Historically, the mana-personality evolves into the hero and the god-like being, whose earthly form is the priest. How very much the doctor is still mana is the whole plaint of the analyst![237]

Mana is a Melanesian word referring to a bewitching or numinous quality in gods and sacred objects. A mana-personality embodies this magical power. In individual psychology, Jung used it to describe the inflationary effect of assimilating autonomous unconscious contents, particularly those associated with anima and animus.

The ego has appropriated something that does not belong to it. But how has it appropriated the mana? If it was really the ego that conquered the anima, then the mana does indeed belong to it, and it would be correct to conclude that one has become important. But why does not this importance, the mana, work upon others? . . . It does not work because one has not in fact become important, but has merely become adulterated with an archetype, another unconscious figure. Hence we must conclude that the ego never conquered the anima at all and therefore has not acquired the mana. All that has happened is a new adulteration.[238]

Mandala. See **quaternity** and **temenos**.

Masculine. See **animus** and **Logos**.

Mechanistic. See **causal, objective level** and **reductive**.

Meditation. A technique of focused **introspection**.
    Jung distinguished between meditation practiced in the East or in traditional Western religious exercises, and its use as a tool for self-understanding, particularly in the realization of projections.

If the ancient art of meditation is practised at all today, it is practised only in religious or philosophical circles, where a theme is subjectively chosen by the meditant or prescribed by an instructor, as in

---

236 "The Mana-Personality," CW 7, par. 377.
237 Ibid., par. 389.
238 Ibid., par. 380.

the Ignatian *Exercitia* or in certain theosophical exercises that developed under Indian influence. These methods are of value only for increasing concentration and consolidating consciousness, but have no significance as regards affecting a synthesis of the personality. On the contrary, their purpose is to shield consciousness from the unconscious and to suppress it.[239]

> When meditation is concerned with the objective products of the unconscious that reach consciousness spontaneously, it unites the conscious with contents that proceed not from a conscious causal chain but from an essentially unconscious process. . . . Part of the unconscious contents is projected, but the projection as such is not recognized. Meditation or critical introspection and objective investigation of the object are needed in order to establish the existence of projections. If the individual is to take stock of himself it is essential that his projections should be recognized, because they falsify the nature of the object and besides this contain items which belong to his own personality and should be integrated with it.[240]

Mother complex. A group of feeling-toned ideas associated with the experience and image of mother.

The mother complex is a potentially active component of everyone's psyche, informed first of all by experience of the personal mother, then by significant contact with other women and by collective assumptions. The constellation of a mother complex has differing effects according to whether it appears in a son or a daughter.

> Typical effects on the son are homosexuality and Don Juanism, and sometimes also impotence [though here the father complex also plays a part]. In homosexuality, the son's entire heterosexuality is tied to the mother in an unconscious form; in Don Juanism, he unconsciously seeks his mother in every woman he meets.[241]

A man's mother complex is influenced by the contrasexual complex, the anima. To the extent that a man establishes a good relationship with his inner woman (instead of being possessed by her), even a negative mother complex may have positive effects.

---

[239] "The Conjunction," CW 14, par. 708.
[240] Ibid., par. 710.
[241] "Psychological Aspects of the Mother Archetype," CW 9i, par. 162.

[He] may have a finely differentiated Eros instead of, or in addition to, homosexuality. . . . This gives him a great capacity for friendship, which often creates ties of astonishing tenderness between men and may even rescue friendship between the sexes from the limbo of the impossible. . . .

In the same way, what in its negative aspect is Don Juanism can appear positively as bold and resolute manliness; ambitious striving after the highest goals; opposition to all stupidity, narrow-mindedness, injustice, and laziness; willingness to make sacrifices for what is regarded as right, sometimes bordering on heroism; perseverance, inflexibility and toughness of will; a curiosity that does not shrink even from the riddles of the universe; and finally, a revolutionary spirit which strives to put a new face upon the world.[242]

In the daughter, the effect of the mother complex ranges from stimulation of the feminine instinct to its inhibition. In the first case, the preponderance of instinct makes the woman unconscious of her own personality.

The exaggeration of the feminine side means an intensification of all female instincts, above all the maternal instinct. The negative aspect is seen in the woman whose only goal is childbirth. To her the husband is . . . first and foremost the instrument of procreation, and she regards him merely as an object to be looked after, along with children, poor relations, cats, dogs, and household furniture.[243]

In the second case, the feminine instinct is inhibited or wiped out altogether.

As a substitute, an overdeveloped Eros results, and this almost invariably leads to an unconscious incestuous relationship with the father. The intensified Eros places an abnormal emphasis on the personality of others. Jealousy of the mother and the desire to outdo her become the leitmotifs of subsequent undertakings.[244]

Alternatively, the inhibition of the feminine instinct may lead a woman to identify with her mother. She is then unconscious of both

---

242 Ibid., pars 164f.
243 Ibid., par. 167.
244 Ibid., par. 168.

her own maternal instinct and her Eros, which are then projected onto the mother.

> As a sort of superwoman (admired involuntarily by the daughter), the mother lives out for her beforehand all that the girl might have lived for herself. She is content to cling to her mother in selfless devotion, while at the same time unconsciously striving, almost against her will, to tyrannize over her, naturally under the mask of complete loyalty and devotion. The daughter leads a shadow-existence, often visibly sucked dry by her mother, and she prolongs her mother's life by a sort of continuous blood transfusion.[245]

Because of their apparent "emptiness," these women are good hooks for men's projections. As devoted and self-sacrificing wives, they often project their own unconscious gifts onto their husbands.

> And then we have the spectacle of a totally insignificant man who seemed to have no chance whatsoever suddenly soaring as if on a magic carpet to the highest summits of achievement.[246]

In Jung's view, these three extreme types are linked together by many intermediate stages, the most important being where there is an overwhelming resistance to the mother and all she stands for.

> It is the supreme example of the negative mother-complex. The motto of this type is: Anything, so long as it is not like Mother! . . . All instinctive processes meet with unexpected difficulties; either sexuality does not function properly, or the children are unwanted, or maternal duties seem unbearable, or the demands of marital life are responded to with impatience and irritation.[247]

Such a woman often excels in Logos activities, where her mother has no place. If she can overcome her merely reactive attitude toward reality, she may later in life come to a deeper appreciation of her femininity.

> Thanks to her lucidity, objectivity, and masculinity, a woman of this type is frequently found in important positions in which her tardily discovered maternal quality, guided by a cool intelligence, ex-

---

245 Ibid., par. 169.
246 Ibid., par. 182.
247 Ibid., par. 170.

erts a most beneficial influence. This rare combination of womanliness and masculine understanding proves valuable in the realm of intimate relationships as well as in practical matters.[248]

At the core of any mother complex is the mother archetype, which means that behind emotional associations with the personal mother, both in men and in women, there is a collective image of nourishment and security on the one hand (the positive mother), and devouring possessiveness on the other (the negative mother).

Motif. See **archetypal image.**

Myth. An involuntary collective statement based on an unconscious psychic experience.

> The primitive mentality does not *invent* myths, it *experiences* them. Myths are original revelations of the preconscious psyche . . . . Many of these unconscious processes may be indirectly occasioned by consciousness, but never by conscious choice. Others appear to arise spontaneously, that is to say, from no discernible or demonstrable conscious cause.[249]

Negative inflation. An unrealistically low opinion of oneself, due to identification with the negative side of the **shadow.** (See also **inflation.**)

> Whenever a sense of moral inferiority appears, it indicates not only a need to assimilate an unconscious component, but also the possibility of such assimilation.[250]

Neurosis. A psychological crisis due to a state of disunity with oneself, or, more formally, a mild **dissociation** of the personality due to the activation of **complexes.** (See also **adaptation, conflict** and **self-regulation of the psyche.**)

> Any incompatibility of character can cause dissociation, and too great a split between the thinking and the feeling function, for in-

---

[248] Ibid., par. 186.
[249] "The Psychology of the Child Archetype," ibid., par. 261.
[250] "The Personal and the Collective Unconscious," CW 7, par. 218.

stance, is already a slight neurosis. When you are not quite at one with yourself . . . you are approaching a neurotic condition.[251]

Every neurosis is characterized by dissociation and conflict, contains complexes, and shows traces of regression and *abaissement.*[252]

Jung's view was that an outbreak of neurosis is purposeful, an opportunity to become conscious of who we are as opposed to who we think we are. By working through the symptoms that invariably accompany neurosis—anxiety, fear, depression, guilt and particularly conflict—we become aware of our limitations and discover our true strengths.

In many cases we have to say, "Thank heaven he could make up his mind to be neurotic." Neurosis is really an attempt at self-cure. . . . It is an attempt of the self-regulating psychic system to restore the balance, in no way different from the function of dreams—only rather more forceful and drastic.[253]

I myself have known more than one person who owed his entire usefulness and reason for existence to a neurosis, which prevented all the worst follies in his life and *forced* him to a mode of living that developed his valuable potentialities. These might have been stifled had not the neurosis, with iron grip, held him to the place where he belonged.[254]

In any breakdown in conscious functioning, energy regresses and unconscious contents are activated in an attempt to compensate the one-sidedness of consciousness.

Neuroses, like all illnesses, are symptoms of maladjustment. Because of some obstacle—a constitutional weakness or defect, wrong education, bad experiences, an unsuitable attitude, etc.—one shrinks from the difficulties which life brings and thus finds oneself back in the world of the infant. The unconscious compensates this regression by producing symbols which, when understood objectively, that is, by means of comparative research, reactivate general ideas that underlie all such natural systems of thought. In this way a change of atti-

---

251 "The Tavistock Lectures," CW 18, par. 383.
252 "Analytical Psychology and Education," CW 17, par. 204.
253 "The Tavistock Lectures," CW 18, par. 389.
254 "The Problem of the Attitude-Type," CW 7, par. 68.

tude is brought about which bridges the dissociation between man as he is and man as he ought to be.[255]

Jung called his attitude toward neurosis energic or final since it was based on the potential progression of energy rather than causal or mechanistic reasons for its regression. The two views are not incompatible but rather complementary: the mechanistic approach looks to the past for the cause of psychic discomfort in the present; Jung focused on the present with an eye to future possibilities.

I no longer seek the cause of a neurosis in the past, but in the present. I ask, what is the necessary task which the patient will not accomplish?[256]

In psychic disturbances it is by no means sufficient in all cases merely to bring the supposed or real causes to consciousness. The treatment involves the integration of contents that have become dissociated from consciousness.[257]

Jung did not dispute Freudian theory that Oedipal fixations can manifest as neurosis in later life. He acknowledged that certain periods in life, and particularly infancy, often have a permanent and determining influence on the personality. But he found this to be an insufficient explanation for those cases in which there was no trace of neurosis until the time of the breakdown.

Freud's sexual theory of neurosis is grounded on a true and factual principle. But it makes the mistake of being one-sided and exclusive; also it commits the imprudence of trying to lay hold of unconfinable Eros with the crude terminology of sex. In this respect Freud is a typical representative of the materialistic epoch, whose hope it was to solve the world riddle in a test-tube.[258]

If the fixation were indeed real [i.e., the primary cause] we should expect to find its influence constant; in other words, a neurosis lasting throughout life. This is obviously not the case. The psychological determination of a neurosis is only partly due to an early infantile

255 "The Philosophical Tree," CW 13, par. 473.
256 "Psychoanalysis and Neurosis," CW4, par. 570.
257 "The Philosophical Tree," CW 13, par. 464.
258 "The Eros Theory," CW 7, par. 33.

predisposition; it must be due to some cause in the present as well. And if we carefully examine the kind of infantile fantasies and occurrences to which the neurotic is attached, we shall be obliged to agree that there is nothing in them that is specifically neurotic. Normal individuals have pretty much the same inner and outer experiences, and may be attached to them to an astonishing degree without developing a neurosis.[259]

What then determines why one person becomes neurotic while another, in similar circumstances, does not? Jung's answer is that the individual psyche knows both its limits and its potential. If the former are being exceeded, or the latter not realized, a breakdown occurs. The psyche itself acts to correct the situation.

There are vast masses of the population who, despite their notorious unconsciousness, never get anywhere near a neurosis. The few who are smitten by such a fate are really persons of the "higher" type who, for one reason or another, have remained too long on a primitive level. Their nature does not in the long run tolerate persistence in what is for them an unnatural torpor. As a result of their narrow conscious outlook and their cramped existence they save energy; bit by bit it accumulates in the unconscious and finally explodes in the form of a more or less acute neurosis.[260]

Jung's view of neurosis differs radically from the classical reductive approach, but it does not substantially change what happens in analysis. Activated fantasies still have to be brought to light, because the energy needed for life is attached to them. The object, however, is not to reveal a supposed root cause of the neurosis but to establish a connection between consciousness and the unconscious that will result in the renewed progression of energy.

Night sea journey. An archetypal motif in mythology, psychologically associated with **depression** and the loss of energy characteristic of **neurosis.**

The night sea journey is a kind of *descensus ad inferos*—a descent into Hades and a journey to the land of ghosts somewhere beyond

---

[259] "Psychoanalysis and Neurosis," CW4, par. 564.
[260] "The Function of the Unconscious," CW 7, par. 291.

this world, beyond consciousness, hence an immersion in the unconscious.[261]

Mythologically, the night sea journey motif usually involves being swallowed by a dragon or sea monster. It is also represented by imprisonment or crucifixion, dismemberment or abduction, experiences traditionally weathered by sun-gods and heroes: Gilgamesh, Osiris, Christ, Dante, Odysseus, Aeneas. In the language of the mystics it is the dark night of the soul.

Jung interpreted such legends symbolically, as illustrations of the regressive movement of energy in an outbreak of neurosis and its potential progression.

> The hero is the symbolical exponent of the movement of libido. Entry into the dragon is the regressive direction, and the journey to the East (the "night sea journey") with its attendant events symbolizes the effort to adapt to the conditions of the psychic inner world. The complete swallowing up and disappearance of the hero in the belly of the dragon represents the complete withdrawal of interest from the outer world. The overcoming of the monster from within is the achievement of adaptation to the conditions of the inner world, and the emergence ("slipping out") of the hero from the monster's belly with the help of a bird, which happens at the moment of sunrise, symbolizes the recommencement of progression.[262]

All the night sea journey myths derive from the perceived behavior of the sun, which, in Jung's lyrical image, "sails over the sea like an immortal god who every evening is immersed in the maternal waters and is born anew in the morning."[263] The sun going down, analogous to the loss of energy in a depression, is the necessary prelude to rebirth. Cleansed in the healing waters (the unconscious), the sun (ego-consciousness) lives again.

Nigredo. An alchemical term, corresponding psychologically to the mental disorientation that typically arises in the process of assimilating unconscious contents, particularly aspects of the **shadow.**

---

[261] "The Psychology of the Transference," CW 16, par. 455.
[262] "On Psychic Energy," CW 8, par. 68.
[263] "Symbols of the Mother and of Rebirth," CW 5, par. 306.

Self-knowledge is an adventure that carries us unexpectedly far and deep. Even a moderately comprehensive knowledge of the shadow can cause a good deal of confusion and mental darkness, since it gives rise to personality problems which one had never remotely imagined before. For this reason alone we can understand why the alchemists called their *nigredo* melancholia, "a black blacker than black," night, an affliction of the soul, confusion, etc., or, more pointedly, the "black raven." For us the raven seems only a funny allegory, but for the medieval adept it was . . . a well-known allegory of the devil.[264]

Numinous. Descriptive of persons, things or situations having a deep emotional resonance, psychologically associated with experiences of the **self.**

Numinous, like numinosity, comes from Latin *numinosum,* referring to a dynamic agency or effect independent of the conscious will.

Religious teaching as well as the *consensus gentium* always and everywhere explain this experience as being due to a cause external to the individual. The *numinosum* is either a quality belonging to a visible object or the influence of an invisible presence that causes a peculiar alteration of consciousness.[265]

Objectivation. A process of **differentiating** the ego from both other persons and contents of the unconscious. (See also **active imagination.**)

Its goal is to detach consciousness from the object so that the individual no longer places the guarantee of his happiness, or of his life even, in factors outside himself, whether they be persons, ideas, or circumstances, but comes to realize that everything depends on whether he holds the treasure or not. If the possession of that gold is realized, then the centre of gravity is *in* the individual and no longer in an object on which he depends.[266]

Jung pointed out that the "treasure" has traditionally been projected onto sacred figures, but that many modern individuals no

---

[264] "The Conjunction," CW 14, par. 741.
[265] "Psychology and Religion," CW 11, par. 6.
[266] "The Tavistock Lectures," CW 18, par. 377.

longer find satisfaction in such historical symbols. They therefore need to find an individual method to "give shape" to the personal complexes and archetypal images.

> For they have to take on form, they have to live their characteristic life, otherwise the individual is severed from the basic function of the psyche [compensation], and then he is neurotic, he is disorientated and in conflict with himself. But if he is able to objectify the impersonal images and relate to them, he is in touch with that vital psychological function which from the dawn of consciousness has been taken care of by religion.[267]

Objective level. An approach to understanding the meaning of images in dreams and fantasies by reference to persons or situations in the outside world. (See also **reductive;** compare **constructive** and **subjective level.**)

> Freud's interpretation of dreams is almost entirely on the objective level, since the dream wishes refer to real objects, or to sexual processes which fall within the physiological, extra-psychological sphere.[268]

Although Jung pioneered the teaching of dream interpretation on the subjective level, where symbolic meaning is paramount, he also recognized the value of the objective approach.

> Enlightening as interpretation on the subjective level may be . . . it may be entirely worthless when a vitally important relationship is the content and cause of the conflict [behind the dream]. Here the dream-figure must be related to the real object. The criterion can always be discovered from the conscious material.[269]

Objective psyche. See **collective unconscious.**

Opposites. Psychologically, the ego and the unconscious. (See also **compensation, conflict, progression** and **transcendent function.**)

---

[267] Ibid., par. 378.
[268] "Definitions," CW 6, par. 779.
[269] "General Aspects of Dream Psychology," CW 8, par. 515.

There is no consciousness without discrimination of opposites.[270]

There is no form of human tragedy that does not in some measure proceed from [the] conflict between the ego and the unconscious.[271]

Whatever attitude exists in the conscious mind, and whichever psychological function is dominant, the opposite is in the unconscious. This situation seldom precipitates a crisis in the first half of life. But for older people who reach an impasse, characterized by a one-sided conscious attitude and the blockage of energy, it is necessary to bring to light psychic contents that have been repressed.

The repressed content must be made conscious so as to produce a tension of opposites, without which no forward movement is possible. The conscious mind is on top, the shadow underneath, and just as high always longs for low and hot for cold, so all consciousness, perhaps without being aware of it, seeks its unconscious opposite, lacking which it is doomed to stagnation, congestion, and ossification. Life is born only of the spark of opposites.[272]

This in turn activates the process of compensation, which leads to an irrational "third," the transcendent function.

Out of [the] collision of opposites the unconscious psyche always creates a third thing of an irrational nature, which the conscious mind neither expects nor understands. It presents itself in a form that is neither a straight "yes" nor a straight "no."[273]

Jung explained the potential renewal of the personality in terms of the principle of entropy in physics, according to which transformations of energy in a relatively closed system take place, and are only possible, as a result of differences in intensity.

Psychologically, we can see this process at work in the development of a lasting and relatively unchanging attitude. After violent oscillations at the beginning the opposites equalize one another, and gradually a new attitude develops, the final stability of which is the greater in proportion to the magnitude of the initial differences. The

---

270 "Psychological Aspects of the Mother Archetype," CW 9i, par. 178.
271 "Analytical Psychology and *Weltanschauung,*" CW 8, par. 706.
272 "The Problem of the Attitude-Type," CW 7, par. 78.
273 "The Psychology of the Child Archetype," CW 9i, par. 285.

greater the tension between the pairs of opposites, the greater will be the energy that comes from them . . . [and] the less chance is there of subsequent disturbances which might arise from friction with material not previously constellated.[274]

Some degree of tension between consciousness and the unconsciousness is both unavoidable and necessary. The aim of analysis is therefore not to eliminate the tension but rather to understand the role it plays in the self-regulation of the psyche. Moreover, the assimilation of unconscious contents results in the ego becoming responsible for what was previously unconscious. There is thus no question of anyone ever being completely at peace.

> The united personality will never quite lose the painful sense of innate discord. Complete redemption from the sufferings of this world is and must remain an illusion. Christ's earthly life likewise ended, not in complacent bliss, but on the cross.[275]

Jung further believed that anyone who attempts to deal with the problem of the opposites on a personal level is making a significant contribution toward world peace.

> The psychological rule says that when an inner situation is not made conscious, it happens outside, as fate. That is to say, when the individual remains undivided and does not become conscious of his inner opposite, the world must perforce act out the conflict and be torn into opposing halves.[276]

Orientation. A term used to indicate the general principle governing a personal **attitude** or viewpoint.

One's psychological orientation determines how one sees and interprets reality. In Jung's model of typology, a thinking attitude is oriented by the principle of logic; a sensation attitude is oriented by the direct perception of concrete facts; intuition orients itself to future possibilities; and feeling is governed by subjective worth. Each of these attitudes may operate in an introverted or extraverted way.

---

[274] "On Psychic Energy," CW 8, par. 49.
[275] "The Psychology of the Transference," CW 16, par. 400.
[276] "Christ, A Symbol of the Self," CW 9ii, par. 126.

Parental complex. A group of emotionally charged images and ideas associated with the parents. (See also **incest.**)

Jung believed that the numinosity surrounding the personal parents, apparent in their more or less magical influence, was to a large extent due to an archetypal image of the primordial parents resident in every psyche.

> The importance that modern psychology attaches to the "parental complex" is a direct continuation of primitive man's experience of the dangerous power of the ancestral spirits. Even the error of judgment which leads him unthinkingly to assume that the spirits are realities of the external world is carried on in our assumption (which is only partially correct) that the real parents are responsible for the parental complex. In the old trauma theory of Freudian psychoanalysis, and in other quarters as well, this assumption even passed for a scientific explanation. (It was in order to avoid this confusion that I advocated the term "parental imago.")[277]

The imago of the parents is composed of both the image created in the individual psyche from the experience of the personal parents and collective elements already present.

> The image is unconsciously projected, and when the parents die, the projected image goes on working as though it were a spirit existing on its own. The primitive then speaks of parental spirits who return by night *(revenants)*, while the modern man calls it a father or mother complex.[278]

> So long as a positive or negative resemblance to the parents is the deciding factor in a love choice, the release from the parental imago, and hence from childhood, is not complete.[279]

Participation mystique. A term derived from anthropology and the study of primitive psychology, denoting a mystical connection, or identity, between subject and object. (See also **archaic, identification** and **projection.**)

---

[277] "The Function of the Unconscious," CW 7, par. 293.
[278] Ibid., par. 294.
[279] "Mind and Earth," CW 10, par. 74.

[Participation mystique] consists in the fact that the subject cannot clearly distinguish himself from the object but is bound to it by a direct relationship which amounts to partial identity. . . . Among civilized peoples it usually occurs between persons, seldom between a person and a thing. In the first case it is a transference relationship . . . . In the second case there is a similar influence on the part of the thing, or else an identification with a thing or the idea of a thing.[280]

[Identity] is a characteristic of the primitive mentality and the real foundation of *participation mystique,* which is nothing but a relic of the original non-differentiation of subject and object, and hence of the primordial unconscious state. It is also a characteristic of the mental state of early infancy, and, finally, of the unconscious of the civilized adult.[281]

Persona. The "I," usually ideal aspects of ourselves, that we present to the outside world.

The persona is . . . a functional complex that comes into existence for reasons of adaptation or personal convenience.[282]

The persona is that which in reality one is not, but which oneself as well as others think one is.[283]

Originally the word persona meant a mask worn by actors to indicate the role they played. On this level, it is both a protective covering and an asset in mixing with other people. Civilized society depends on interactions between people through the persona.

There are indeed people who lack a developed persona . . . blundering from one social solecism to the next, perfectly harmless and innocent, soulful bores or appealing children, or, if they are women, spectral Cassandras dreaded for their tactlessness, eternally misunderstood, never knowing what they are about, always taking forgiveness for granted, blind to the world, hopeless dreamers. From them we can see how a neglected persona works.[284]

---

[280] "Definitions," CW 6, par. 781.
[281] Ibid., par. 741.
[282] Ibid., par. 801.
[283] "Concerning Rebirth," CW 9i, par. 221.
[284] "Anima and Animus," CW 7, par. 318.

Before the persona has been differentiated from the ego, the persona is experienced as individuality. In fact, as a social identity on the one hand and an ideal image on the other, there is little individual about it.

> It is, as its name implies, only a mask of the collective psyche, a mask that *feigns individuality,* making others and oneself believe that one is individual, whereas one is simply acting a role through which the collective psyche speaks.
>
> When we analyse the persona we strip off the mask, and discover that what seemed to be individual is at bottom collective; in other words, that the persona was only a mask of the collective psyche. Fundamentally the persona is nothing real: it is a compromise between individual and society as to what a man should appear to be. He takes a name, earns a title, exercises a function, he is this or that. In a certain sense all this is real, yet in relation to the essential individuality of the person concerned it is only a secondary reality, a compromise formation, in making which others often have a greater share than he.[285]

A psychological understanding of the persona as a function of relationship to the outside world makes it possible to assume and drop one at will. But by rewarding a particular persona, the outside world invites identification with it. Money, respect and power come to those who can perform single-mindedly and well in a social role. From being a useful convenience, therefore, the persona may become a trap and a source of neurosis.

> A man cannot get rid of himself in favour of an artificial personality without punishment. Even the attempt to do so brings on, in all ordinary cases, unconscious reactions in the form of bad moods, affects, phobias, obsessive ideas, backsliding vices, etc. The social "strong man" is in his private life often a mere child where his own states of feeling are concerned.[286]

> The demands of propriety and good manners are an added inducement to assume a becoming mask. What goes on behind the mask is then called "private life." This painfully familiar division of conscious

---

[285] "The Persona as a Segment of the Collective Psyche," ibid., pars. 245f.
[286] "Anima and Animus," ibid., par. 307.

ness into two figures, often preposterously different, is an incisive psychological operation that is bound to have repercussions on the unconscious.[287]

Among the consequences of identifying with a persona are: we lose sight of who we are without a protective covering; our reactions are predetermined by collective expectations (we do and think and feel what our persona "should" do, think and feel); those close to us complain of our emotional distance; and we cannot imagine life without it.

To the extent that ego-consciousness is identified with the persona, the neglected inner life (personified in the shadow and anima or animus) is activated in compensation. The consequences, experienced in symptoms characteristic of neurosis, can stimulate the process of individuation.

There is, after all, something individual in the peculiar choice and delineation of the persona, and . . . despite the exclusive identity of the ego-consciousness with the persona the unconscious self, one's real individuality, is always present and makes itself felt indirectly if not directly. Although the ego-consciousness is at first identical with the persona—that compromise role in which we parade before the community—yet the unconscious self can never be repressed to the point of extinction. Its influence is chiefly manifest in the special nature of the contrasting and compensating contents of the unconscious. The purely personal attitude of the conscious mind evokes reactions on the part of the unconscious, and these, together with personal repressions, contain the seeds of individual development.[288]

Personal unconscious. The personal layer of the **unconscious,** distinct from the **collective unconscious.**

The personal unconscious contains lost memories, painful ideas that are repressed (i.e., forgotten on purpose), subliminal perceptions, by which are meant sense-perceptions that were not strong enough to reach consciousness, and finally, contents that are not yet ripe for consciousness.[289]

---

[287] Ibid., par. 305.

[288] "The Persona as a Segment of the Collective Psyche," ibid., par. 247.

[289] "The Personal and the Collective Unconscious," ibid., par. 103.

Personality. Aspects of the **soul** as it functions in the world. (See also **individuality.**)

For the development of personality, differentiation from collective values, particularly those embodied in and adhered to by the persona, is essential.

A change from one milieu to another brings about a striking alteration of personality, and on each occasion a clearly defined character emerges that is noticeably different from the previous one. . . . The social character is oriented on the one hand by the expectations and demands of society, and on the other by the social aims and aspirations of the individual. The domestic character is, as a rule, moulded by emotional demands and an easy-going acquiescence for the sake of comfort and convenience; when it frequently happens that men who in public life are extremely energetic, spirited, obstinate, wilful and ruthless appear good-natured, mild, compliant, even weak, when at home and in the bosom of the family. Which is the true character, the real personality? . . .

. . . . In my view the answer to the above question should be that such a man has no real character at all: he is not individual but collective, the plaything of circumstance and general expectations. Were he individual, he would have the same character despite the variation of attitude. He would not be identical with the attitude of the moment, and he neither would nor could prevent his individuality from expressing itself just as clearly in one state as in another.[290]

Personification. The tendency of psychic contents or **complexes** to take on a distinct personality, separate from the ego.

Every autonomous or even relatively autonomous complex has the peculiarity of appearing as a personality, i.e., of being personified. This can be observed most readily in the so-called spiritualistic manifestations of automatic writing and the like. The sentences produced are always personal statements and are propounded in the first person singular, as though behind every utterance there stood an actual personality. A naïve intelligence at once thinks of spirits.[291]

The ego may also deliberately personify unconscious contents or

---

[290] "Definitions," CW 6, pars. 798f.
[291] "Anima and Animus," CW 7, par. 312.

the affects that arise from them, using the method of active imagination, in order to facilitate communication between consciousness and the unconscious.

Philosophers' stone. In alchemy, a metaphor for the successful transmutation of base metal into gold; psychologically, an archetypal image of **wholeness**. (See also **coniunctio**.)

Jung quoted from the *Rosarium philosophorum:*

> Make a round circle of man and woman, extract therefrom a quadrangle and from it a triangle. Make the circle round, and you will have the Philosophers' Stone.[292]

Possession. A term used to describe the **identification** of consciousness with an unconscious content or **complex**.

The most common forms of possession are by the shadow and the contrasexual complexes, anima/animus.

> A man who is possessed by his shadow is always standing in his own light and falling into his own traps. Whenever possible, he prefers to make an unfavorable impression on others. . . .
> Possession caused by the anima or animus presents a different picture. . . . In the state of possession both figures lose their charm and their values; they retain them only when they are turned away from the world, in the introverted state, when they serve as bridges to the unconscious. Turned towards the world, the anima is fickle, capricious, moody, uncontrolled and emotional, sometimes gifted with daemonic intuitions, ruthless, malicious, untruthful, bitchy, double-faced, and mystical. The animus is obstinate, harping on principles, laying down the law, dogmatic, world-reforming, theoretic, word-mongering, argumentative, and domineering. Both alike have bad taste: the anima surrounds herself with inferior people, and the animus lets himself be taken in by second-rate thinking.[293]

Power complex. A group of emotionally toned ideas associated with an attitude that seeks to subordinate all influences and experience to the supremacy of the personal ego.

---

[292] "Psychology and Religion," CW 11, par. 92.
[293] "Concerning Rebirth," CW 9i, pars. 222f.

Prima materia. An alchemical term meaning "original matter," used psychologically to denote both the instinctual foundation of life and the raw material one works with in analysis—dreams, emotions, conflicts, etc.

Primary function. The psychological function that is most differentiated. (Compare **inferior function.**)

In Jung's model of typology, the primary or superior function is the one we automatically use because it comes most naturally.

> Experience shows that it is practically impossible, owing to adverse circumstances in general, for anyone to develop all his psychological functions simultaneously. The demands of society compel a man to apply himself first and foremost to the differentiation of the function with which he is best equipped by nature, or which will secure him the greatest social success. Very frequently, indeed as a general rule, a man identifies more or less completely with the most favoured and hence the most developed function. It is this that gives rise to the various psychological types.[294]

In deciding which of the four functions—thinking, feeling, sensation or intuition—is primary, one must closely observe which function is more or less completely under conscious control, and which functions have a haphazard or random character. The superior function (which can manifest in either an introverted or an extraverted way) is always more highly developed than the others, which possess infantile and primitive traits.

> The superior function is always an expression of the conscious personality, of its aims, will, and general performance, whereas the less differentiated functions fall into the category of things that simply "happen" to one.[295]

Primitive. Descriptive of the original, or undifferentiated, human psyche. (See also **archaic.**)

> I use the term "primitive" in the sense of "primordial," and . . . do not imply any kind of value judgment. Also, when I speak of a

---

[294] "Definitions," CW 6, par. 763.
[295] "General Description of the Types," ibid., par. 575.

"vestige" of a primitive state, I no not necessarily mean that this state will sooner or later come to an end. On the contrary, I see no reason why it should not endure as long as humanity lasts.[296]

Primordial image. See **archetypal image.**

Progression. The daily advance of the process of psychological **adaptation,** the opposite of **regression.** (See also **neurosis.**)

> Progression is a forwards movement of life in the same sense that time moves forwards. This movement can occur in two different forms: either extraverted, when the progression is predominantly influenced by objects and environmental conditions, or introverted, when it has to adapt itself to the conditions of the ego (or, more accurately, of the "subjective factor"). Similarly, regression can proceed along two lines: either as a retreat from the outside world (introversion), or as a flight into extravagant experience of the outside world (extraversion). Failure in the first case drives a man into a state of dull brooding, and in the second case into leading the life of a wastrel.[297]

In the normal course of life, there is a relatively easy progression of libido; energy may be directed more or less at will. This is not the same as psychological development or individuation. Progression refers simply to the continuous flow or current of life. It is commonly interrupted by a conflict or the inability to adapt to changing circumstances.

> During the progression of libido the pairs of opposites are united in the co-ordinated flow of psychic processes. . . . But in the stoppage of libido that occurs when progression has become impossible, positive and negative can no longer unite in co-ordinated action, because both have attained an equal value which keeps the scales balanced.[298]

The struggle between the opposites would continue unabated if the process of regression, the backward movement of libido, did not set in, its purpose being to compensate the conscious attitude.

---

[296] "A Review of the Complex Theory," CW 8, par. 218.
[297] "On Psychic Energy," ibid., par. 77.
[298] Ibid., par. 61.

Through their collision the opposites are gradually deprived of value and depotentiated.... In proportion to the decrease in value of the conscious opposites there is an increase in value of all those psychic processes which are not concerned with outward adaptation and therefore are seldom or never employed consciously.[299]

As the energic value of these previously unconscious psychic processes increases, they manifest indirectly as disturbances of conscious behavior and symptoms characteristic of neurosis. Prominent aspects of the psyche one then needs to become aware of are the persona, the contrasexual complex (anima/animus) and the shadow.

Projection. An automatic process whereby contents of one's own unconscious are perceived to be in others. (See also **archaic, identification** and **participation mystique.**)

Just as we tend to assume that the world is as we see it, we naïvely suppose that people are as we imagine them to be.... All the contents of our unconscious are constantly being projected into our surroundings, and it is only by recognizing certain properties of the objects as projections or imagos that we are able to distinguish them from the real properties of the objects.... *Cum grano salis,* we always see our own unavowed mistakes in our opponent. Excellent examples of this are to be found in all personal quarrels. Unless we are possessed of an unusual degree of self-awareness we shall never see through our projections but must always succumb to them, because the mind in its natural state presupposes the existence of such projections. It is the natural and given thing for unconscious contents to be projected.[300]

Projection means the expulsion of a subjective content into an object; it is the opposite of introjection. Accordingly, it is a process of dissimilation, by which a subjective content becomes alienated from the subject and is, so to speak, embodied in the object. The subject gets rid of painful, incompatible contents by projecting them.[301]

Projection is not a conscious process. One meets with projections, one does not make them.

---

299 "On Psychic Energy," ibid., par. 62.
300 "General Aspects of Dream Psychology," ibid., par. 507.
301 "Definitions," CW 6, par. 783.

The general psychological reason for projection is always an activated unconscious that seeks expression.[302]

It is possible to project certain characteristics onto another person who does not possess them at all, but the one being projected upon may unconsciously encourage it.

It frequently happens that the object offers a hook to the projection, and even lures it out. This is generally the case when the object himself (or herself) is not conscious of the quality in question: in that way it works directly upon the unconscious of the projicient. *For all projections provoke counter-projections* when the object is unconscious of the quality projected upon it by the subject.[303]

Through projection one can create a series of imaginary relationships that often have little or nothing to do with the outside world.

The effect of projection is to isolate the subject from his environment, since instead of a real relation to it there is now only an illusory one. Projections change the world into the replica of one's own unknown face. In the last analysis, therefore, they lead to an autoerotic or autistic condition in which one dreams a world whose reality remains forever unattainable.[304]

Projection also has positive effects. In everyday life it facilitates interpersonal relations. In addition, when we assume that some quality or characteristic is present in another, and then, through experience, find that this is not so, we can learn something about ourselves. This involves withdrawing or dissolving projections.

So long as the libido can use these projections as agreeable and convenient bridges to the world, they will alleviate life in a positive way. But as soon as the libido wants to strike out on another path, and for this purpose begins running back along the previous bridges of projection, they will work as the greatest hindrances it is possible to imagine, for they effectively prevent any real detachment from the former object.[305]

---

302 "The Tavistock Lectures," CW 18, par. 352.
303 "General Aspects of Dream Psychology," CW 8, par. 519.
304 "The Shadow," CW 9ii, par. 17.
305 "General Aspects of Dream Psychology," CW 8, par. 507.

The need to withdraw projections is generally signaled by frustrated expectations in relationships, accompanied by strong affect. But Jung believed that until there is an obvious discordance between what we imagine to be true and the reality we are presented with, there is no need to speak of projections, let alone withdraw them.

> Projection . . . is properly so called only when the need to dissolve the identity with the object has already arisen. This need arises when the identity becomes a disturbing factor, i.e., when the absence of the projected content is a hindrance to adaptation and its withdrawal into the subject has become desirable. From this moment the previous partial identity acquires the character of projection. The term projection therefore signifies a state of identity that has become noticeable.[306]

Jung distinguished between *passive* projection and *active* projection. Passive projection is completely automatic and unintentional, like falling in love. The less we know about another person, the easier it is to passively project unconscious aspects of ourselves onto them.

Active projection is better known as empathy—we feel ourselves into the other's shoes. Empathy that extends to the point where we lose our own standpoint becomes identification.

The projection of the personal shadow generally falls on persons of the same sex. On a collective level, it gives rise to war, scapegoating and confrontations between political parties. Projection that takes place in the context of a therapeutic relationship is called transference or countertransference, depending on whether the analysand or the analyst is the one projecting.

In terms of the contrasexual complexes, anima and animus, projection is both a common cause of animosity and a singular source of vitality.

> When animus and anima meet, the animus draws his sword of power and the anima ejects her poison of illusion and seduction. The outcome need not always be negative, since the two are equally likely to fall in love.[307]

---

[306] "Definitions," CW 6, par. 783.
[307] "The Syzygy: Anima and Animus," CW 9ii, par. 30.

Provisional life. A term used to describe an attitude toward life that is more or less imaginary, not rooted in the here and now, commonly associated with **puer** psychology.

Psyche. The totality of all psychological processes, both conscious and unconscious.

> The psyche is far from being a homogenous unit—on the contrary, it is a boiling cauldron of contradictory impulses, inhibitions, and affects, and for many people the conflict between them is so insupportable that they even wish for the deliverance preached by theologians.[308]

The way in which the psyche manifests is a complicated interplay of many factors, including an individual's age, sex, hereditary disposition, psychological type and attitude, and degree of conscious control over the instincts.

> Psychic processes . . . behave like a scale along which consciousness "slides." At one moment it finds itself in the vicinity of instinct, and falls under its influence; at another, it slides along to the other end where spirit predominates and even assimilates the instinctual processes most opposed to it.[309]

The tremendous complexity of psychic phenomena led Jung to the belief that attempts to formulate a comprehensive theory of the psyche were doomed to failure.

> The premises are always far too simple. The psyche is the starting-point of all human experience, and all the knowledge we have gained eventually leads back to it. The psyche is the beginning and end of all cognition. It is not only the object of its science, but the subject also. This gives psychology a unique place among all the other sciences: on the one hand there is a constant doubt as to the possibility of its being a science at all, while on the other hand psychology acquires the right to state a theoretical problem the solution of which will be one of the most difficult tasks for a future philosophy.[310]

---

[308] "Psychological Aspects of the Mother Archetype," CW 9i, par. 190.
[309] "On the Nature of the Psyche," CW 8, par. 408.
[310] "Psychological Factors in Human Behaviour," ibid., par. 261.

Psychic energy. See **libido.**

Psychization. The process of **reflection** whereby an **instinct** or unconscious content is made conscious.

Psychogenic. Descriptive of mental disturbances having a psychological rather than physiological origin.

> Nobody doubts that the neuroses are *psychogenic*. "Psychogenesis" means that the essential cause of a neurosis, or the condition under which it arises, is of a psychic nature. It may, for instance, be a psychic shock, a gruelling conflict, a wrong kind of psychic adaptation, a fatal illusion, and so on.[311]

Psychoid. A concept applicable to virtually any archetype, expressing the essentially unknown but experienceable connection between psyche and matter.

> Psyche is essentially conflict between blind instinct and will (freedom of choice). Where instinct predominates, *psychoid* processes set in which pertain to the sphere of the unconscious as elements incapable of consciousness. The psychoid process is not the unconscious as such, for this has a far greater extension.[312]

> It seems to me probable that the real nature of the archetype is not capable of being made conscious, that it is transcendent, on which account I call it psychoid.[313]

Psychological types. See **type** and **typology.**

Psychopomp. A psychic factor that mediates unconscious contents to consciousness, often personified in the image of a wise old man or woman, and sometimes as a helpful animal.

Psychosis. An extreme **dissociation** of the personality.

Like neurosis, a psychotic condition is due to the activity of unconscious complexes and the phenomenon of splitting. In neurosis,

---

[311] "Mental disease and the Psyche," CW 3, par. 496.
[312] "On the Nature of the Psyche," CW 8, par. 380.
[313] Ibid., par. 417.

the complexes are only relatively autonomous. In psychosis, they are completely disconnected from consciousness.

> To have complexes is in itself normal; but if the complexes are incompatible, that part of the personality which is too contrary to the conscious part becomes split off. If the split reaches the organic structure, the dissociation is a psychosis, a schizophrenic condition, as the term denotes. Each complex then lives an existence of its own, with no personality left to tie them together.[314]

> [In schizophrenia] the split-off figures assume banal, grotesque, or highly exaggerated names and characters, and are often objectionable in many other ways. They do not, moreover, co-operate with the patient's consciousness. They are not tactful and they have no respect for sentimental values. On the contrary, they break in and make a disturbance at any time, they torment the ego in a hundred ways; all are objectionable and shocking, either in their noisy and impertinent behaviour or in their grotesque cruelty and obscenity. There is an apparent chaos of incoherent visions, voices, and characters, all of an overwhelmingly strange and incomprehensible nature.[315]

Jung believed that many psychoses, and particularly schizophrenia, were psychogenic, resulting from an *abaissement du niveau mental* and an ego too weak to resist the onslaught of unconscious contents. He reserved judgment on whether biological factors were a contributing cause.

Puer aeternus. Latin for "eternal child," used in mythology to designate a child-god who is forever young; psychologically it refers to an older man whose emotional life has remained at an adolescent level, usually coupled with too great a dependence on the mother.[316]

The puer typically leads a provisional life, due to the fear of being caught in a situation from which it might not be possible to escape. His lot is seldom what he really wants and one day he will do something about it—but not just yet. Plans for the future slip away in fantasies of what will be, what could be, while no decisive action is

---

[314] "The Tavistock Lectures," CW 18, par. 382.
[315] "On the Psychogenesis of Schizophrenia," CW 3, par. 508.
[316] The term puella is used when referring to a woman, though one might also speak of a puer animus—or a puella anima.

taken to change. He covets independence and freedom, chafes at boundaries and limits, and tends to find any restriction intolerable.

> [The world] makes demands on the masculinity of a man, on his ardour, above all on his courage and resolution when it comes to throwing his whole being into the scales. For this he would need a faithless Eros, one capable of forgetting his mother and undergoing the pain of relinquishing the first love of his life.[317]

Common symptoms of puer psychology are dreams of imprisonment and similar imagery: chains, bars, cages, entrapment, bondage. Life itself, existential reality, is experienced as a prison. The bars are unconscious ties to the unfettered world of early life.

The puer's shadow is the senex (Latin for "old man"), associated with the god Apollo—disciplined, controlled, responsible, rational, ordered. Conversely, the shadow of the senex is the puer, related to Dionysus—unbounded instinct, disorder, intoxication, whimsy.

Whoever lives out one pattern to the exclusion of the other risks constellating the opposite. Hence individuation quite as often involves the need for a well-controlled person to get closer to the spontaneous, instinctual life as it does the puer's need to grow up.

> The "eternal child" in man is an indescribable experience, an incongruity, a handicap, and a divine prerogative; an imponderable that determines the ultimate worth or worthlessness of a personality.[318]

Quaternity. An image with a four-fold structure, usually square or circular and symmetrical; psychologically, it points to the idea of **wholeness.** (See also **temenos.**)

> The quaternity is one of the most widespread archetypes and has also proved to be one of the most useful schemata for representing the arrangement of the functions by which the conscious mind takes its bearings.[319] It is like the crossed threads in the telescope of our understanding. The cross formed by the points of the quaternity is no less universal and has in addition the highest possible moral and religious significance for Western man. Similarly the circle, as the

---

[317] "The Syzygy: Anima and Animus," CW 9ii, par. 22.
[318] "The Psychology of the Child Archetype," CW 9i, par. 300.
[319] See below, **typology.**

symbol of completeness and perfect being, is a widespread expression for heaven, sun, and God; it also expresses the primordial image of man and the soul.[320]

From the circle and quaternity motif is derived the symbol of the geometrically formed crystal and the wonder-working stone. From here analogy formation leads on to the city, castle, church, house, and vessel. Another variant is the wheel *(rota)*. The former motif emphasizes the ego's containment in the greater dimension of the self; the latter emphasizes the rotation which also appears as a ritual circumambulation. Psychologically, it denotes concentration on and preoccupation with a centre.[321]

Jung believed that the spontaneous production of quaternary images (including mandalas), whether consciously or in dreams and fantasies, can indicate the ego's capacity to assimilate unconscious material. But they may also be essentially apotropaic, an attempt by the psyche to prevent itself from disintegrating.

These images are naturally only anticipations of a wholeness which is, in principle, always just beyond our reach. Also, they do not invariably indicate a subliminal readiness on the part of the patient to realize that wholeness consciously, at a later stage; often they mean no more than a temporary compensation of chaotic confusion.[322]

Rapport. A feeling of agreement between oneself and others.

It frequently happens that despite an absolute difference of standpoint a rapport nevertheless comes about, and in the following way: one party, by unspoken projection, assumes that the other is, in all essentials, of the same opinion as himself, while the other divines or senses an objective community of interest, of which, however, the former has no conscious inkling and whose existence he would at once dispute, just as it would never occur to the other that his relationship should be based on a common point of view. A rapport of this kind is by far the most frequent; it rests on mutual projection, which later becomes the source of many misunderstandings.[323]

---

320 "The Psychology of the Transference," CW 16, par. 405.

321 "The Structure and Dynamics of the Self," CW 9ii, par. 352.

322 "The Psychology of the Transference," CW 16, par. 536.

323 "General Description of the Types," CW 6, par. 618.

Rational. Descriptive of thoughts, feelings and actions that accord with reason, an attitude based on objective values established by practical experience. (Compare **irrational.**)

> The rational attitude which permits us to declare objective values as valid at all is not the work of the individual subject, but the product of human history.
>
> Most objective values—and reason itself—are firmly established complexes of ideas handed down through the ages. Countless generations have laboured at their organization with the same necessity with which the living organism reacts to the average, constantly recurring environmental conditions, confronting them with corresponding functional complexes, as the eye, for instance, perfectly corresponds to the nature of light. . . . Thus the laws of reason are the laws that designate and govern the average, "correct," adapted attitude. Everything is "rational" that accords with these laws, everything that contravenes them is "irrational."[324]

Jung described the psychological functions of thinking and feeling as rational because they are decisively influenced by reflection.

Rebirth. A process experienced as a renewal or transformation of the personality. (See also **individuation.**)

> Rebirth is not a process that we can in any way observe. We can neither measure nor weigh nor photograph it. It is entirely beyond sense perception. . . . One speaks of rebirth; one professes rebirth; one is filled with rebirth. . . . We have to be content with its psychic reality.[325]

Jung distinguished between five different forms of rebirth: *metempsychosis* (transmigration of souls), *reincarnation* (in a human body), *resurrection, psychological rebirth* (individuation) and indirect change that comes about through *participation in the process of transformation.*

Psychological rebirth was Jung's particular focus. Induced by ritual or stimulated by immediate personal experience, it results in an enlargement of the personality. He acknowledged that one might feel

---

[324] "Definitions," ibid., par. 785f.
[325] "Concerning Rebirth," CW 9i, par. 206.

transformed during certain group experiences, but he cautioned against confusing this with genuine rebirth.

> If any considerable group of persons are united and identified with one another by a particular frame of mind, the resultant transformation experience bears only a very remote resemblance to the experience of individual transformation. A group experience takes place on a lower level of consciousness than the experience of an individual. This is due to the fact that, when many people gather together to share one common emotion, the total psyche emerging from the group is below the level of the individual psyche. If it is a very large group, the collective psyche will be more like the psyche of an animal . . . .
>
> . . . The group experience goes no deeper than the level of one's own mind in that state. It does work a change in you, but the change does not last.[326]

Reductive. Literally, "leading back," descriptive of interpretations of **dreams** and **neurosis** in terms of events in outer life, particularly those in childhood. (Compare **constructive** and **final**.)

> The reductive method is oriented backwards, in contrast to the constructive method . . . . The interpretive methods of both Freud and Adler are reductive, since in both cases there is a reduction to the elementary processes of wishing or striving, which in the last resort are of an infantile or physiological nature. . . . Reduction has a disintegrative effect on the real significance of the unconscious product, since this is either traced back to its historical antecedents [e.g., childhood] and thereby annihilated, or integrated once again with the same elementary process from which it arose.[327]

In dream interpretation, the reductive (also called mechanistic) method seeks to explain images of persons and situations in terms of concrete reality. The constructive or final approach focuses on the dream's symbolic content.

Although Jung himself concentrated on the constructive approach, he regarded reductive analysis as an important first step in the treatment of psychological problems, particularly in the first half of life.

---

[326] Ibid., pars. 225f.
[327] "Definitions," CW 6, par. 788.

The neuroses of the young generally come from a collision between the forces of reality and an inadequate, infantile attitude, which from the causal point of view is characterized by an abnormal dependence on the real or imaginary parents, and from the teleological point of view by unrealizable fictions, plans, and aspirations. Here the reductive methods of Freud and Adler are entirely in place.[328]

Reflection. Mental activity that concentrates on a particular content of consciousness, an instinct encompassing religion and the search for meaning.

Ordinarily we do not think of "reflection" as ever having been instinctive, but associate it with a conscious state of mind. *Reflexio* means "bending back" and, used psychologically, would denote the fact that the reflex which carries the stimulus over into its instinctive discharge is interfered with by psychization. . . . Thus in place of the compulsive act there appears a certain degree of freedom, and in place of predictability a relative unpredictability as to the effect of the impulse.[329]

In Jung's view, the richness of the human psyche and its essential character are determined by the reflective instinct.

Reflection is the cultural instinct *par excellence,* and its strength is shown in the power of culture to maintain itself in the face of untamed nature.[330]

Regression. The backward movement of libido to an earlier mode of **adaptation,** often accompanied by infantile fantasies and wishes. (See also **depression;** compare **progression.**)

Regression . . . as an adaptation to the conditions of the inner world, springs from the vital need to satisfy the demands of individuation.[331]

What robs Nature of its glamour, and life of its joy, is the habit of looking back for something that used to be outside, instead of look-

---

[328] "The Problem of the Attitude-Type," CW 7, par. 88.
[329] "Psychological Factors in Human Behaviour," CW 8, par. 241.
[330] Ibid., par. 243.
[331] "On Psychic Energy," ibid., par. 75.

ing inside, into the depths of the depressive state. This looking back leads to regression and is the first step along that path. Regression is also an involuntary introversion in so far as the past is an object of memory and therefore a psychic content, an endopsychic factor. It is a relapse into the past caused by a depression in the present.[332]

Jung believed that the blockage of the forward movement of energy is due to the inability of the dominant conscious attitude to adapt to changing circumstances. However, the unconscious contents thereby activated contain the seeds of a new progression. For instance, the opposite or inferior function is waiting in the wings, potentially capable of modifying the inadequate conscious attitude.

If thinking fails as the adapted function, because it is dealing with a situation to which one can adapt only by feeling, then the unconscious material activated by regression will contain the missing feeling function, although still in embryonic form, archaic and undeveloped. Similarly, in the opposite type, regression would activate a thinking function that would effectively compensate the inadequate feeling.[333]

The regression of energy confronts us with the problem of our own psychology. From the final point of view, therefore, regression is as necessary in the developmental process as is progression.

Regarded causally, regression is determined, say, by a "mother fixation." But from the final standpoint the libido regresses to the *imago* of the mother in order to find there the memory associations by means of which further development can take place, for instance from a sexual system into an intellectual or spiritual system.

The first explanation exhausts itself in stressing the importance of the cause and completely overlooks the final significance of the regressive process. From this angle the whole edifice of civilization becomes a mere substitute for the impossibility of incest. But the second explanation allows us to foresee what will follow from the regression, and at the same time it helps us to understand the significance of the memory-images that have been reactivated.[334]

---

[332] "The Sacrifice," CW 5, par. 625.
[333] "On Psychic Energy," CW 8, par. 65.
[334] Ibid., pars. 43f.

Jung believed that behind the mundane symptoms of regression lay its symbolic meaning: the need for psychological renewal, reflected in mythology as the journey of the hero.

> It is precisely the strongest and best among men, the heroes, who give way to their regressive longing and purposely expose themselves to the danger of being devoured by the monster of the maternal abyss. But if a man is a hero, he is a hero because, in the final reckoning, he did not let the monster devour him, but subdued it, not once but many times. Victory over the collective psyche alone yields the true value—the capture of the hoard, the invincible weapon, the magic talisman, or whatever it be that the myth deems most desirable.[335]

Regressive restoration of the persona. A term used to describe what can happen when there has been a major collapse in the conscious attitude.

> Take as an example a businessman who takes too great a risk and consequently goes bankrupt. If he does not allow himself to be discouraged by this depressing experience, but, undismayed, keeps his former daring, perhaps with a little salutary caution added, his wound will be healed without permanent injury. But if, on the other hand, he goes to pieces, abjures all further risks, and laboriously tries to patch up his social reputation within the confines of a much more limited personality, doing inferior work with the mentality of a scared child, in a post far below him, then, technically speaking, he will have restored his persona in a regressive way. . . . Formerly perhaps he wanted more than he could accomplish; now he does not even dare to attempt what he has it in him to do.[336]

> The regressive restoration of the persona is a possible course only for the man who owes the critical failure of his life to his own inflatedness. With diminished personality, he turns back to the measure he can fill. But in every other case resignation and self-belittlement are an evasion, which in the long run can be kept up only at the cost of neurotic sickliness.[337]

---

[335] "The Relations between the Ego and the Unconscious," CW 7, par. 261.
[336] Ibid., par. 254.
[337] Ibid., par. 259.

Religious attitude. Psychologically, an attitude informed by the careful observation of, and respect for, invisible forces and personal experience.

> We might say . . . that the term "religion" designates the attitude peculiar to a consciousness which has been changed by experience of the *numinosum*.[338]

> Religion . . . is an *instinctive* attitude peculiar to man, and its manifestations can be followed all through human history.[339]

The religious attitude is quite different from faith associated with a specific creed. The latter, as a codified and dogmatized form of an original religious experience, simply gives expression to a particular collective belief. True religion involves a subjective relationship to certain metaphysical, extramundane factors.

> A creed is a confession of faith intended chiefly for the world at large and is thus an intramundane affair, while the meaning and purpose of religion lie in the relationship of the individual to God (Christianity, Judaism, Islam) or to the path of salvation and liberation (Buddhism).[340]

Jung believed that a neurosis in the second half of life is seldom cured without the development of a religious attitude, prompted by a spontaneous revelation of the spirit.

> This spirit is an autonomous psychic happening, a hush that follows the storm, a reconciling light in the darkness of man's mind, secretly bringing order into the chaos of his soul.[341]

Repression. The unconscious suppression of psychic contents that are incompatible with the attitude of consciousness.

> Repression is a process that begins in early childhood under the moral influence of the environment and continues through life.[342]

---

[338] "Psychology and Religion," CW 11, par. 9.
[339] "The Undiscovered Self," CW 10, par. 512.
[340] Ibid., par. 507.
[341] "A Psychological Approach to the Trinity," CW 11, par. 260.
[342] "The Personal and the Collective Unconscious," CW 7, par. 202.

Repression causes what is called a *systematic amnesia,* where only specific memories or groups of ideas are withdrawn from recollection. In such cases a certain attitude or tendency can be detected on the part of the conscious mind, a deliberate intention to avoid even the bare possibility of recollection, for the very good reason that it would be painful or disagreeable.[343]

Repression is not only a factor in the etiology of many neuroses, it also determines contents of the personal shadow, since the ego generally represses material that would disturb peace of mind

In the course of development following puberty, consciousness is confronted with affective tendencies, impulses, and fantasies which for a variety of reasons it is not willing or not able to assimilate. It then reacts with repression in various forms, in the effort to get rid of the troublesome intruders. The general rule is that the more negative the conscious attitude is, and the more it resists, devalues, and is afraid, the more repulsive, aggressive, and frightening is the face which the dissociated content assumes.[344]

Many repressed contents come to the surface naturally during the analytic process. Where there are strong resistances to uncovering repressed material, Jung believed these should always be respected lest the ego be overwhelmed.

The general rule should be that the weakness of the conscious attitude is proportional to the strength of the resistance. When, therefore, there are strong resistances, the conscious rapport with the patient must be carefully watched, and—in certain cases—his conscious attitude must be supported to such a degree that, in view of later developments, one would be bound to charge oneself with the grossest inconsistency. That is inevitable, because one can never be too sure that the weak state of the patient's conscious mind will prove equal to the subsequent assault of the unconscious. In fact, one must go on supporting his conscious (or, as Freud thinks, "repressive") attitude until the patient can let the "repressed" contents rise up spontaneously.[345]

---

343 "Analytical Psychology and Education," CW 17, par. 199a.
344 "The Philosophical Tree," CW 13, par. 464.
345 "The Psychology of the Unconscious," CW 16, par. 381.

Sacred marriage. See **coniunctio.**

Sacrifice. Psychologically, associated with the need to give up the world of childhood, often signaled by the **regression** of energy.

> One must give up the retrospective longing which only wants to resuscitate the torpid bliss and effortlessness of childhood.[346]

> For him who looks backwards the whole world, even the starry sky, becomes the mother who bends over him and enfolds him on all sides, and from the renunciation of this image, and of the longing for it, arises the picture of the world as we know it today.[347]

Schizophrenia. See **psychosis.**

Self. The archetype of **wholeness** and the regulating center of the psyche; a transpersonal power that transcends the ego.

> As an empirical concept, the self designates the whole range of psychic phenomena in man. It expresses the unity of the personality as a whole. But in so far as the total personality, on account of its unconscious component, can be only in part conscious, the concept of the self is, in part, only *potentially* empirical and is to that extent a *postulate.* In other words, it encompasses both the experienceable and the inexperienceable (or the not yet experienced). . . . It is a *transcendental* concept, for it presupposes the existence of unconscious factors on empirical grounds and thus characterizes an entity that can be described only in part.[348]

> The self is not only the centre, but also the whole circumference which embraces both conscious and unconscious; it is the centre of this totality, just as the ego is the centre of consciousness.[349]

Like any archetype, the essential nature of the self is unknowable, but its manifestations are the content of myth and legend.

> The self appears in dreams, myths, and fairytales in the figure of the "supraordinate personality," such as a king, hero, prophet, saviour,

---

[346] "The Sacrifice," CW 5, par. 643.
[347] Ibid., par. 646.
[348] "Definitions," CW 6, par. 789.
[349] "Introduction," CW 12, par. 44.

etc., or in the form of a totality symbol, such as the circle, square, *quadratura circuli,* cross, etc. When it represents a *complexio oppositorum,* a union of opposites, it can also appear as a united duality, in the form, for instance, of *tao* as the interplay of *yang* and *yin,* or of the hostile brothers, or of the hero and his adversary (arch-enemy, dragon), Faust and Mephistopheles, etc. Empirically, therefore, the self appears as a play of light and shadow, although conceived as a totality and unity in which the opposites are united.[350]

The realization of the self as an autonomous psychic factor is often stimulated by the irruption of unconscious contents over which the ego has no control. This can result in neurosis and a subsequent renewal of the personality, or in an inflated identification with the greater power.

The ego cannot help discovering that the afflux of unconscious contents has vitalized the personality, enriched it and created a figure that somehow dwarfs the ego in scope and intensity. . . . Naturally, in these circumstances there is the greatest temptation simply to follow the power-instinct and to identify the ego with the self outright, in order to keep up the illusion of the ego's mastery. . . . [But] the self has a functional meaning only when it can act compensatorily to ego-consciousness. If the ego is dissolved in identification with the self, it gives rise to a sort of nebulous superman with a puffed-up ego.[351]

Experiences of the self possess a numinosity characteristic of religious revelations. Hence Jung believed there was no essential difference between the self as an experiential, psychological reality and the traditional concept of a supreme deity.

It might equally be called the "God within us."[352]

Self-regulation of the psyche. A concept based on the compensatory relationship between consciousness and the unconscious. (See also **adaptation, compensation, neurosis, opposites** and **transcendent function.**)

---

[350] "Definitions," CW 6, par. 790.

[351] "On the Nature of the Psyche," CW 8, par. 430.

[352] "The Mana-Personality," CW 7, par. 399.

The psyche does not merely *react,* it gives its own specific answer to the influences at work upon it.[353]

The process of self-regulation is going on all the time within the psyche. It only becomes noticeable when ego-consciousness has particular difficulty in adapting to external or internal reality. That is often the start of a process, proceeeding along the lines outlined in the chart, that may lead to individuation.

The Self-regulation of the Psyche

1. Difficulty of adaptation. Little progression of libido.

2. Regression of energy (depression, lack of disposable energy).

3. Activation of unconscious contents (fantasies, complexes, archetypal images, inferior function, opposite attitude, shadow, anima/animus, etc.). Compensation.

4. Symptoms of neurosis (confusion, fear, anxiety, guilt, moods, extreme affect, etc.).

5. Unconscious or half-conscious conflict between ego and contents activated in the unconscious. Inner tension. Defensive reactions.

6. Activation of the transcendent function, involving the self and archetypal patterns of wholeness.

7. Formation of symbols (numinosity, synchronicity).

8. Transfer of energy between unconscious contents and consciousness. Enlargement of the ego, progression of energy.

9. Assimilation of unconscious contents. Individuation.

Consciousness and the unconscious seldom agree as to their contents and their tendencies. The self-regulating activities of the psyche, manifest in dreams, fantasies and synchronistic experiences, attempt to correct any significant imbalance. According to Jung, this is necessary for several reasons:

---

[353] "Some Crucial Points in Psychoanalysis," CW 4, par. 665.

(1) Consciousness possesses a threshold intensity which its contents must have attained, so that all elements that are too weak remain in the unconscious.

(2) Consciousness, because of its directed functions, exercises an inhibition (which Freud calls censorship) on all incompatible material, with the result that it sinks into the unconscious.

(3) Consciousness constitutes the momentary process of adaptation, whereas the unconscious contains not only all the forgotten material of the individual's own past, but all the inherited behaviour traces constituting the structure of the mind [i.e., archetypes].

(4) The unconscious contains all the fantasy combinations which have not yet attained the threshold intensity, but which in the course of time and under suitable conditions will enter the light of consciousness.[354]

Sensation. The psychological **function** that perceives immediate reality through the physical senses. (Compare **intuition.**)

> An attitude that seeks to do justice to the unconscious as well as to one's fellow human beings cannot possibly rest on knowledge alone, in so far as this consists merely of thinking and intuition. It would lack the function that perceives values, i.e., feeling, as well as the *fonction du réel,* i.e., sensation, the sensible perception of reality.[355]

In Jung's model of typology, sensation, like intuition, is an irrational function. It perceives concrete facts, with no judgment of what they mean or what they are worth.

> Sensation must be strictly differentiated from feeling, since the latter is an entirely different process, although it may associate itself with sensation as "feeling-tone." Sensation is related not only to external stimuli but to inner ones, i.e., to changes in the internal organic processes.[356]

Jung also distinguished between sensuous or concrete sensation and abstract sensation.

---

354 "The Transcendent Function," CW 8, par. 132.
355 "The Psychology of the Transference," CW 16, par. 486.
356 "Definitions," CW 6, par. 792.

Concrete sensation never appears in "pure" form, but is always mixed up with ideas, feelings, thoughts. . . . The concrete sensation of a flower . . . conveys a perception not only of the flower as such, but also of the stem, leaves, habitat, and so on. It is also instantly mingled with feeling of pleasure or dislike which the sight of the flower evokes, or with simultaneous olfactory perceptions, or with thoughts about its botanical classification, etc. But abstract sensation immediately picks out the most salient sensuous attribute of the flower, its brilliant redness, for instance, and makes this the sole or at least the principle content of consciousness, entirely detached from all other admixtures. Abstract sensation is found chiefly among artists. Like every abstraction, it is a product of functional differentiation.[357]

Shadow. Hidden or unconscious aspects of oneself, both good and bad, which the ego has either repressed or never recognized. (See also **repression.**)

The shadow is a moral problem that challenges the whole ego-personality, for no one can become conscious of the shadow without considerable moral effort. To become conscious of it involves recognizing the dark aspects of the personality as present and real.[358]

Before unconscious contents have been differentiated, the shadow is in effect the whole of the unconscious. It is commonly personified in dreams by persons of the same sex as the dreamer.

The shadow is composed for the most part of repressed desires and uncivilized impulses, morally inferior motives, childish fantasies and resentments, etc.—all those things about oneself one is not proud of. These unacknowledged personal characteristics are often experienced in others through the mechanism of projection.

Although, with insight and good will, the shadow can to some extent be assimilated into the conscious personality, experience shows that there are certain features which offer the most obstinate resistance to moral control and prove almost impossible to influence. These resistances are usually bound up with *projections,* which are not recognized as such, and their recognition is a moral achievement

---

[357] Ibid., par. 794.
[358] "The Shadow," CW 9ii, par. 14.

beyond the ordinary. While some traits peculiar to the shadow can be recognized without too much difficulty as one's personal qualities, in this case both insight and good will are unavailing because the cause of the emotion appears to lie, beyond all possibility of doubt, in the *other person.*[359]

The realization of the shadow is inhibited by the persona. To the degree that we identify with a bright persona, the shadow is correspondingly dark. Thus shadow and persona stand in a compensatory relationship, and the conflict between them is invariably present in an outbreak of neurosis. The characteristic depression at such times indicates the need to realize that one is not all one pretends or wishes to be.

There is no generally effective technique for assimilating the shadow. It is more like diplomacy or statesmanship and it is always an individual matter. First one has to accept and take seriously the existence of the shadow. Second, one has to become aware of its qualities and intentions. This happens through conscientious attention to moods, fantasies and impulses. Third, a long process of negotiation is unavoidable.

It is a therapeutic necessity, indeed, the first requisite of any thorough psychological method, for consciousness to confront its shadow. In the end this must lead to some kind of union, even though the union consists at first in an open conflict, and often remains so for a long time. It is a struggle that cannot be abolished by rational means. When it is wilfully repressed it continues in the unconscious and merely expresses itself indirectly and all the more dangerously, so no advantage is gained. The struggle goes on until the opponents run out of breath. What the outcome will be can never be seen in advance. The only certain thing is that both parties will be changed.[360]

This process of coming to terms with the Other in us is well worth while, because in this way we get to know aspects of our nature which we would not allow anybody else to show us and which we ourselves would never have admitted.[361]

---

[359] Ibid., par. 16.
[360] "Rex and Regina," CW 14, par. 514.
[361] "The Conjunction," ibid., par. 706.

Responsibility for the shadow rests with the ego. That is why the shadow is a moral problem. It is one thing to realize what it looks like—what we are capable of. It is quite something else to determine what we can live out, or with.

> Confrontation with the shadow produces at first a dead balance, a standstill that hampers moral decisions and makes convictions ineffective or even impossible. Everything becomes doubtful.[362]

The shadow is not, however, only the dark underside of the personality. It also consists of instincts, abilities and positive moral qualities that have long been buried or never been conscious.

> The shadow is merely somewhat inferior, primitive, unadapted, and awkward; not wholly bad. It even contains childish or primitive qualities which would in a way vitalize and embellish human existence, but—convention forbids![363]

> If it has been believed hitherto that the human shadow was the source of all evil, it can now be ascertained on closer investigation that the unconscious man, that is, his shadow, does not consist only of morally reprehensible tendencies, but also displays a number of good qualities, such as normal instincts, appropriate reactions, realistic insights, creative impulses, etc.[364]

An outbreak of neurosis constellates both sides of the shadow: those qualities and activities one is not proud of, and new possibilities one never knew were there.

Jung distinguished between the personal and the collective or archetypal shadow.

> With a little self-criticism one can see through the shadow—so far as its nature is personal. But when it appears as an archetype, one encounters the same difficulties as with anima and animus. In other words, it is quite within the bounds of possibility for a man to recognize the relative evil of his nature, but it is a rare and shattering experience for him to gaze into the face of absolute evil.[365]

---

362 Ibid., par. 708.
363 "Psychology and Religion," CW 11, par. 134.
364 "Conclusion," CW 9ii, par. 423.
365 "The Shadow," ibid., par. 19.

Soul. A functional complex in the psyche. (See also **Eros, Logos** and **soul-image.**)

While Jung often used the word soul in its traditional theological sense, he strictly limited its psychological meaning.

> I have been compelled, in my investigations into the structure of the unconscious, to make a conceptual distinction between *soul* and *psyche*. By psyche I understand the totality of all psychic processes, conscious as well as unconscious. By soul, on the other hand, I understand a clearly demarcated functional complex that can best be described as a "personality."[366]

With this understanding, Jung outlined partial manifestations of the soul in terms of anima/animus and persona. In his later writing on the transference, informed by his study of the alchemical *opus*—which Jung understood as psychologically analogous to the individuation process—he was more specific.

> The "soul" which accrues to ego-consciousness during the *opus* has a feminine character in the man and a masculine character in a woman. His anima wants to reconcile and unite; her animus tries to discern and discriminate.[367]

Soul-image. The representation, in dreams or other products of the unconscious, of the inner personality, usually contrasexual. (See also **anima** and **animus.**)

> Wherever an impassioned, almost magical, relationship exists between the sexes, it is invariably a question of a projected soul-image. Since these relationships are very common, the soul must be unconscious just as frequently.[368]

The soul-image is a specific archetypal image produced by the unconscious, commonly experienced in projection onto a person of the opposite sex.

> For an idealistic woman, a depraved man is often the bearer of the soul-image; hence the "saviour-fantasy" so frequent in such cases.

---

[366] "Definitions," CW 6, par. 797
[367] "The Psychology of the Transference," CW 16, par. 522.
[368] "Definitions," CW 6, par. 809.

The same thing happens with men, when the prostitute is surrounded with the halo of a soul crying for succour.[369]

Where consciousness itself is identified with the soul, the soul-image is more likely to be an aspect of the persona.

In that event, the persona, being unconscious, will be projected on a person of the same sex, thus providing a foundation for many cases of open or latent homosexuality, and of father-transferences in men or mother-transferences in women. In such cases there is always a defective adaptation to external reality and a lack of relatedness, because identification with the soul produces an attitude predominantly oriented to the perception of inner processes.[370]

Many relationships begin and initially thrive on the basis of projected soul-images. Inherently symbiotic, they often end badly.

Spirit. An archetype and a functional complex, often **personified** and experienced as enlivening, analogous to what the **archaic** mind felt to be an invisible, breathlike "presence."

Spirit, like God, denotes an object of psychic experience which cannot be proved to exist in the external world and cannot be understood rationally. This is its meaning if we use the word "spirit" in its best sense.[371]

The archetype of spirit in the shape of a man, hobgoblin, or animal always appears in a situation where insight, understanding, good advice, determination, planning, etc., are needed but cannot be mustered on one's own resources. The archetype compensates this state of spiritual deficiency by contents designed to fill the gap.[372]

Jung was careful to distinguish between spirit as a psychological concept and its traditional use in religion.

From the psychological point of view, the phenomenon of spirit, like every autonomous complex, appears as an intention of the unconscious superior to, or at least on a par with, intentions of the

---

369 Ibid., par. 811.
370 Ibid., par. 809.
371 "Spirit and Life," CW 8, par. 626.
372 "The Phenomenology of the Spirit in Fairytales," CW 9i, par. 398.

ego. If we are to do justice to the essence of the thing we call spirit, we should really speak of a "higher" consciousness rather than of the unconscious.[373]

The common modern idea of spirit ill accords with the Christian view, which regards it as the *summum bonum,* as God himself. To be sure, there is also the idea of an evil spirit. But the modern idea cannot be equated with that either, since for us spirit is not necessarily evil; we would have to call it morally indifferent or neutral.[374]

Splitting. A term used to describe the **dissociation** of the personality, marked by attitudes and behavior patterns determined by **complexes.** (See also **neurosis.**)

Although this peculiarity is most clearly observable in psychopathology, fundamentally it is a normal phenomenon, which can be recognized with the greatest ease in the projections made by the primitive psyche. The tendency to split means that parts of the psyche detach themselves from consciousness to such an extent that they not only appear foreign but lead an autonomous life of their own. It need not be a question of hysterical multiple personality, or schizophrenic alterations of personality, but merely of so-called "complexes" that come entirely within the scope of the normal.[375]

Subjective level. The approach to dreams and other images where the persons or situations pictured are seen as symbolic representations of factors belonging entirely to the subject's own psyche. (Compare **objective level.**)

Interpretation of an unconscious product on the subjective level reveals the presence of subjective judgments and tendencies of which the object is made the vehicle. When, therefore, an object-imago appears in an unconscious product, it is not on that account the image of a real object; it is far more likely that we are dealing with a subjective functional complex. Interpretation on the subjective level allows us to take a broader psychological view not only of dreams but also of literary works, in which the individual figures then appear as

---

373 "Spirit and Life," CW 8, par. 643.

374 "The Phenomenology of the Spirit in Fairytales," CW 9i, par. 394.

375 "Psychological Factors in Human Behaviour," CW 8, par. 253.

representatives of relatively autonomous functional complexes in the psyche of the author.[376]

In the analytic process, the main task after the reductive interpretation of images thrown up by the unconscious is to understand what they say about oneself.

> To establish a really mature attitude, he has to see the *subjective value* of all these images which seem to create trouble for him. He has to assimilate them into his own psychology; he has to find out in what way they are part of himself; how he attributes for instance a positive value to an *object,* when as a matter of fact it is he who could and should develop this value. And in the same way, when he projects negative qualities and therefore hates and loathes the object, he has to discover that he is projecting his own inferior side, his shadow, as it were, because he prefers to have an optimistic and one-sided image of himself.[377]

Subjective psyche. See **personal unconscious.**

Subtle body. The somatic unconscious, a transcendental concept involving the relationship between mind and body.

> The part of the unconscious which is designated as the subtle body becomes more and more identical with the functioning of the body, and therefore it grows darker and darker and ends in the utter darkness of matter. . . . Somewhere our unconscious becomes material, because the body is the living unit, and our conscious and our unconscious are embedded in it: they contact the body. Somewhere there is a place where the two ends meet and become interlocked. And that is the [subtle body] where one cannot say whether it is matter, or what one calls "psyche."[378]

Superior function. See **primary function.**

Supraordinate personality. An aspect of the psyche superior to, and transcending, the **ego.** (See also **self.**)

---

376 "Definitions," CW 6, par. 813.
377 "The Tavistock Lectures," CW 18, par. 367.
378 *Nietzsche's Zarathustra,* vol. 1, p. 441.

The "supraordinate personality" is the total man, i.e., man as he really is, not as he appears to himself. . . .

I usually describe the supraordinate personality as the "self," thus making a sharp distinction between the ego, which, as is well known, extends only as far as the conscious mind, and the *whole* of the personality, which includes the unconscious as well as the conscious component. The ego is thus related to the self as part to whole. To that extent the self is supraordinate.[379]

Symbiosis. A psychological state where contents of one's personal unconscious are experienced in another person. (See also **projection** and **soul-image.**)

Symbiosis manifests in unconscious interpersonal bonds, easily established and difficult to break. Jung gave an example in terms of introversion and extraversion. Where one of these attitudes is dominant, the other, being unconscious, is automatically projected.

Either type has a predilection to marry its opposite, each being unconsciously complementary to the other. . . . The one takes care of reflection and the other sees to the initiative and practical action. When the two types marry, they may effect an ideal union. So long as they are fully occupied with their adaptation to the manifold external needs of life they fit together admirably.[380]

Problems in such relationships typically surface only later in life, accompanied by strong affect.

When the man has made enough money, or if a fine legacy should drop from the skies and external necessity no longer presses, then they have time to occupy themselves with one another. Hitherto they stood back to back and defended themselves against necessity. But now they turn face to face and look for understanding—only to discover that they have never understood one another. Each speaks a different language. Then the conflict between the two types begins. This struggle is envenomed, brutal, full of mutual depreciation, even when conducted quietly and in the greatest intimacy. For the value of the one is the negation of value for the other.[381]

---

379 "The Psychological Aspects of the Kore," CW 9i, pars. 314f.
380 "The Problem of the Attitude-Type," CW 7, par. 80.
381 Ibid.

The ending of a symbiotic relationship often precipitates an outbreak of neurosis, stimulated by an inner need to assimilate those aspects of oneself that were projected onto the partner.

Symbol. The best possible expression for something unknown. (See also **constructive** and **final.**)

> Every psychological expression is a symbol if we assume that it states or signifies something more and other than itself which eludes our present knowledge.[382]

Jung distinguished between a symbol and a sign. Insignia on uniforms, for instance, are not symbols but signs that identify the wearer. In dealing with unconscious material (dreams, fantasies, etc.), the images can be interpreted semiotically, as symptomatic signs pointing to known or knowable facts, or symbolically, as expressing something essentially unknown.

> The interpretation of the cross as a symbol of divine love is *semiotic,* because "divine love" describes the fact to be expressed better and more aptly than a cross, which can have many other meanings. On the other hand, an interpretation of the cross is *symbolic* when it puts the cross beyond all conceivable explanations, regarding it as expressing an as yet unknown and incomprehensible fact of a mystical or transcendent, i.e., psychological, nature, which simply finds itself most appropriately represented in the cross.[383]

Whether something is interpreted as a symbol or a sign depends mainly on the attitude of the observer. Jung linked the semiotic and symbolic approaches, respectively, to the causal and final points of view. He acknowledged the importance of both.

> Psychic development cannot be accomplished by intention and will alone; it needs the attraction of the symbol, whose value quantum exceeds that of the cause. But the formation of a symbol cannot take place until the mind has dwelt long enough on the elementary facts, that is to say until the inner or outer necessities of the life-process have brought about a transformation of energy.[384]

---

[382] "Definitions," CW 6, par. 817.
[383] Ibid., par. 815.
[384] "On Psychic Energy," CW 8, par. 47.

The symbolic attitude is at bottom constructive, in that it gives priority to understanding the meaning or purpose of psychological phenomena, rather than seeking a reductive explanation.

> There are, of course, neurotics who regard their unconscious products, which are mostly morbid symptoms, as symbols of supreme importance. Generally, however, this is not what happens. On the contrary, the neurotic of today is only too prone to regard a product that may actually be full of significance as a mere "symptom."[385]

Jung's primary interest in symbols lay in their ability to transform and redirect instinctive energy.

> How are we to explain religious processes, for instance, whose nature is essentially symbolical? In abstract form, symbols are religious ideas; in the form of action, they are rites or ceremonies. They are the manifestation and expression of excess libido. At the same time they are stepping-stones to new activities, which must be called cultural in order to distinguish them from the instinctual functions that run their regular course according to natural law.[386]

The formation of symbols is going on all the time within the psyche, appearing in fantasies and dreams. In analysis, after reductive explanations have been exhausted, symbol-formation is reinforced by the constructive approach. The aim is to make instinctive energy available for meaningful work and a productive life.

Synchronicity. A phenomenon where an event in the outside world coincides meaningfully with a psychological state of mind.

> Synchronicity . . . consists of two factors: *a)* An unconscious image comes into consciousness either directly (i.e., literally) or indirectly (symbolized or suggested) in the form of a dream, idea, or premonition. *b)* An objective situation coincides with this content. The one is as puzzling as the other.[387]

Jung associated synchronistic experiences with the relativity of space and time and a degree of unconsciousness.

---

385 "Definitions, CW 6, par. 821.
386 "On Psychic Energy," CW 8, par. 91.
387 "Synchronicity: An Acausal Connecting Principle," ibid., par. 858.

The very diverse and confusing aspects of these phenomena are, so far as I can see at present, completely explicable on the assumption of a psychically relative space-time continuum. As soon as a psychic content crosses the threshold of consciousness, the synchronistic marginal phenomena disappear, time and space resume their accustomed sway, and consciousness is once more isolated in its subjectivity. . . . Conversely, synchronistic phenomena can be evoked by putting the subject into an unconscious state.[388]

Synchronicity was defined by Jung as an "acausal connecting principle," an essentially mysterious connection between the personal psyche and the material world, based on the fact that at bottom they are only different forms of energy.

It is not only possible but fairly probable, even, that psyche and matter are two different aspects of one and the same thing. The synchronicity phenomena point, it seems to me, in this direction, for they show that the nonpsychic can behave like the psychic, and vice versa, without there being any causal connection between them.[389]

Synthetic. See constructive.

Temenos. A Greek word meaning a sacred, protected space; psychologically, descriptive of both a personal container and the sense of privacy that surrounds an analytical relationship.

Jung believed that the need to establish or preserve a temenos is often indicated by drawings or dream images of a quaternary nature, such as mandalas.

The symbol of the mandala has exactly this meaning of a holy place, a *temenos,* to protect the centre. And it is a symbol which is one of the most important motifs in the objectivation of unconscious images. It is a means of protecting the centre of the personality from being drawn out and from being influenced from outside.[390]

Tertium non datur. The reconciling "third," not logically foreseeable, characteristic of a resolution in a **conflict** situation when the

---

[388] "On the Nature of the Psyche," CW 8, par. 440.
[389] Ibid., par. 418.
[390] "The Tavistock Lectures," CW 18, par. 410.

tension between **opposites** has been held in consciousness. (See also **transcendent function.**)

> As a rule it occurs when the analysis has constellated the opposites so powerfully that a union or synthesis of the personality becomes an imperative necessity. . . . [This situation] requires a real solution and necessitates a third thing in which the opposites can unite. Here the logic of the intellect usually fails, for in a logical antithesis there is no third. The "solvent" can only be of an irrational nature. In nature the resolution of opposites is always an energic process: she acts *symbolically* in the truest sense of the word, doing something that expresses both sides, just as a waterfall visibly mediates between above and below.[391]

Thinking. The mental process of interpreting what is perceived. (Compare **feeling.**)

In Jung's model of typology, thinking is one of the four functions used for psychological orientation. Along with feeling, it is a rational function. If thinking is the primary function, then feeling is automatically the inferior function.

> Thinking, if it is to be real thinking and true to its own principle, must rigorously exclude feeling. This, of course, does not do away with the the fact that there are individuals whose thinking and feeling are on the same level, both being of equal motive power for consciousness. But in these cases there is also no question of a differentiated type, but merely of relatively undeveloped thinking and feeling.[392]

As a process of apperception, thinking may be active or passive.

> Active thinking is an act of the *will,* passive thinking is a mere occurrence. In the former case, I submit the contents of ideation to a voluntary act of judgment; in the latter, conceptual connections establish themselves of their own accord, and judgments are formed that may even contradict my intention. . . . Active thinking, accordingly, would correspond to my concept of *directed thinking.* Passive thinking . . . I would call . . . *intuitive* thinking.[393]

---

[391] "The Conjunction," CW 14, par. 705.
[392] "General Description of the Types," CW 6, par. 667.
[393] "Definitions," ibid., par. 830.

The capacity for directed thinking I call *intellect;* the capacity for passive or undirected thinking I call *intellectual intuition.*[394]

Transcendent function. A psychic function that arises from the tension between consciousness and the unconscious and supports their union. (See also **opposites** and **tertium non datur.**)

> When there is full parity of the opposites, attested by the ego's absolute participation in both, this necessarily leads to a suspension of the will, for the will can no longer operate when every motive has an equally strong countermotive. Since life cannot tolerate a standstill, a damming up of vital energy results, and this would lead to an insupportable condition did not the tension of opposites produce a new, uniting function that transcends them. This function arises quite naturally from the regression of libido caused by the blockage.[395]

> The tendencies of the conscious and the unconscious are the two factors that together make up the transcendent function. It is called "transcendent" because it makes the transition from one attitude to another organically possible.[396]

In a conflict situation, or a state of depression for which there is no apparent reason, the development of the transcendent function depends on becoming aware of unconscious material. This is most readily available in dreams, but because they are so difficult to understand Jung considered the method of active imagination—giving "form" to dreams, fantasies, etc.—to be more useful.

> Once the unconscious content has been given form and the meaning of the formulation is understood, the question arises as to how the ego will relate to this position, and how the ego and the unconscious are to come to terms. This is the second and more important stage of the procedure, the bringing together of opposites for the production of a third: the transcendent function. At this stage it is no longer the unconscious that takes the lead, but the ego.[397]

---

[394] Ibid., par. 832.
[395] Ibid., par. 824.
[396] "The Transcendent Function," CW 8, par. 145.
[397] Ibid., par. 181.

This process requires an ego that can maintain its standpoint in face of the counterposition of the unconscious. Both are of equal value. The confrontation between the two generates a tension charged with energy and creates a living, third essence.

> From the activity of the unconscious there now emerges a new content, constellated by thesis and antithesis in equal measure and standing in a compensatory relation to both. It thus forms the middle ground on which the opposites can be united. If, for instance, we conceive the opposition to be sensuality versus spirituality, then the mediatory content born out of the unconscious provides a welcome means of expression for the spiritual thesis, because of its rich spiritual associations, and also for the sensual antithesis, because of its sensuous imagery. The ego, however, torn between thesis and antithesis, finds in the middle ground its own counterpart, its sole and unique means of expression, and it eagerly seizes on this in order to be delivered from its division.[398]

The transcendent function is essentially an aspect of the self-regulation of the psyche. It typically manifests symbolically and is experienced as a new attitude toward oneself and life.

> If the mediatory product remains intact, it forms the raw material for a process not of dissolution but of construction, in which thesis and antithesis both play their part. In this way it becomes a new content that governs the whole attitude, putting an end to the division and forcing the energy of the opposites into a common channel. The standstill is overcome and life can flow on with renewed power towards new goals.[399]

Transference. A particular case of **projection,** used to describe the unconscious, emotional bond that arises in the analysand toward the analyst. (See also **countertransference**.)

> Unconscious contents are invariably projected at first upon concrete persons and situations. Many projections can ultimately be integrated back into the individual once he has recognized their subjective origin; others resist integration, and although they may be de-

---

[398] "Definitions," CW 6, par. 825.
[399] Ibid., par. 827.

tached from their original objects, they thereupon transfer themselves to the doctor. Among these contents the relation to the parent of opposite sex plays an important part, i.e., the relation of son to mother, daughter to father, and also that of brother to sister.[400]

Once the projections are recognized as such, the particular form of rapport known as the transference is at an end, and the problem of individual relationship begins.[401]

A transference may be either positive or negative; the former is marked by feelings of affection and respect, the latter by hostility and resistance.

For one type of person (called the infantile-rebel) a positive transference is, to begin with, an important achievement with a healing significance; for the other (the infantile-obedient) it is a dangerous backsliding, a convenient way of evading life's duties. For the first a negative transference denotes increased insubordination, hence a backsliding and an evasion of life's duties, for the second it is a step forward with a healing significance.[402]

Jung did not regard the transference merely as a projection of infantile-erotic fantasies. Though these may be present at the beginning of analysis, they can be dissolved through the reductive method. Then the *purpose* of the transference becomes the main issue and guide.

An exclusively sexual interpretation of dreams and fantasies is a shocking violation of the patient's psychological material: infantile-sexual fantasy is by no means the whole story, since the material also contains a creative element, the purpose of which is to shape a way out of the neurosis.[403]

Although Jung made contradictory statements about the therapeutic importance of the transference—for instance:

The transference phenomenon is an inevitable feature of every thorough analysis, for it is imperative that the doctor should get into the

---

[400] "The Psychology of the Transference," CW 16, par. 357.
[401] "The Therapeutic Value of Abreaction," ibid., par. 287.
[402] "Some Crucial Points in Psychoanalysis," CW 4, par. 659.
[403] "The Therapeutic Value of Abreaction," CW 16, par. 277.

closest possible touch with the patient's line of psychological development.[404]

We do not work *with* the "transference to the analyst," but *against it and in spite of it.*[405]

A transference is always a hindrance; it is never an advantage.[406]

Medical treatment of the transference gives the patient a priceless opportunity to withdraw his projections, to make good his losses, and to integrate his personality.[407]

—he did not doubt its significance when it was present.

The suitably trained analyst mediates the transcendent function for the patient, i.e., helps him to bring conscious and unconscious together and so arrive at a new attitude. . . . The patient clings by means of the transference to the person who seems to promise him a renewal of attitude; through it he seeks this change, which is vital to him, even though he may not be conscious of doing so. For the patient, therefore, the analyst has the character of an indispensable figure absolutely necessary for life.[408]

Whatever is unconscious in the analysand and needed for healthy functioning is projected onto the analyst. This includes archetypal images of wholeness, with the result that the analyst takes on the stature of a mana-personality. The analysand's task is then to understand such images on the subjective level, a primary aim being to constellate the patient's own inner analyst.

Empathy is an important purposive element in the transference. By means of empathy the analysand attempts to emulate the presumably healthier attitude of the analyst, and thereby to attain a better level of adaptation.

The patient is bound to the analyst by ties of affection or resistance and cannot help following and imitating his psychic attitude. By this means he feels his way along (empathy). And with the best will in

[404] Ibid., par. 283.
[405] "Some Crucial Points in Psychoanalysis," CW 4, par. 601.
[406] "The Tavistock Lectures," CW 18, par. 349.
[407] "The Psychology of the Transference," CW 16, par. 420.
[408] "The Transcendent Function," CW 8, par. 146.

the world and for all his technical skill the analyst cannot prevent it, for empathy works surely and instinctively in spite of conscious judgment, be it never so strong.[409]

Jung believed that analyzing the transference was extremely important in order to return projected contents necessary for the individuation of the analysand. But he pointed out that even after projections have been withdrawn there remains a strong connection between the two parties. This is because of an instinctive factor that has few outlets in modern society: kinship libido.

> Everyone is now a stranger among strangers. Kinship libido—which could still engender a satisfying feeling of belonging together, as for instance in the early Christian communities—has long been deprived of its object. But, being an instinct, it is not to be satisfied by any mere substitute such as a creed, party, nation, or state. It wants the *human* connection. That is the core of the whole transference phenomenon, and it is impossible to argue it away, because relationship to the self is at once relationship to our fellow man, and no one can be related to the latter until he is related to himself.[410]

Transformation. See rebirth.

Trauma. An intense emotional shock, often accompanied by **repression** and a **splitting** of the personality. (See **abreaction**).

Treasure hard to attain. Broadly, a reference to aspects of self-knowledge necessary for psychological **individuality;** specifically, a metaphor for the goal of **individuation,** a good working relationship with the **self.**

Trickster. Psychologically, descriptive of unconscious **shadow** tendencies of an ambivalent, mercurial nature.

> [The trickster] is a forerunner of the saviour . . . . He is both subhuman and superhuman, a bestial and divine being, whose chief and most alarming characteristic is his unconsciousness.[411]

---

[409] "Some Crucial Points in Psychoanalysis," CW 4, par. 661.

[410] "The Psychology of the Transference," CW 16, par. 445.

[411] "On the Psychology of the Trickster-Figure," CW 9i, par. 472,

The so-called civilized man has forgotten the trickster. He remembers him only figuratively and metaphorically, when, irritated by his own ineptitude, he speaks of fate playing tricks on him or of things being bewitched. He never suspects that his own hidden and apparently harmless shadow has qualities whose dangerousness exceeds his wildest dreams.[412]

Type. A characteristic general **attitude** or **function.**

[The] *function-types,* which one can call the thinking, feeling, sensation, and intuitive types, may be divided into two classes according to the quality of the basic function, i.e., into the rational and the irrational. The thinking and feeling types belong to the former class, the sensation and intuitive types to the latter. A further division into two classes is permitted by the predominant trend of the movement of libido, namely introversion and extraversion.[413]

Jung believed that the early distortion of type due to parental or other environmental influences can lead to neurosis in later life.

As a rule, whenever such a falsification of type takes place . . . the individual becomes neurotic later, and can be cured only by developing the attitude consonant with his nature.[414]

Typology. A system in which individual attitudes and behavior patterns are categorized in an attempt to explain the differences between people.

Jung's model of typology grew out of an extensive historical review of the type question in literature, mythology, aesthetics, philosophy and psychopathology. Whereas earlier classifications were based on observations of temperamental or physiological behavior patterns, Jung's model is concerned with the movement of energy and the way in which one habitually or preferentially orients oneself in the world.

First and foremost, it is a critical tool for the research worker, who needs definite points of view and guidelines if he is to reduce the

---

[412] Ibid., par. 478.

[413] "Definitions," CW 6, par. 835.

[414] "General Description of the Types," ibid., par. 560.

chaotic profusion of individual experiences to any kind of order. . . .
Secondly, a typology is a great help in understanding the wide varia-
tions that occur among individuals, and it also furnishes a clue to the
fundamental differences in the psychological theories now current.
Last but not least, it is an essential means for determining the
"personal equation" of the practising psychologist, who, armed with
an exact knowledge of his differentiated and inferior functions, can
avoid many serious blunders in dealing with his patients.[415]

Jung differentiated eight typological groups: two personality attitudes—introversion and extraversion—and four functions—thinking, sensation, intuition and feeling, each of which may operate in an
introverted or extraverted way.

Introversion and extraversion are psychological modes of adaptation. In the former, the movement of energy is toward the inner
world. In the latter, interest is directed toward the outer world. In
one case the subject (inner reality) and in the other the object (things
and other people, outer reality) is of primary importance.

> [Introversion] is normally characterized by a hesitant, reflective, retir-
> ing nature that keeps itself to itself, shrinks from objects, is always
> slightly on the defensive and prefers to hide behind mistrustful scru-
> tiny. [Extraversion] is normally characterized by an outgoing, candid,
> and accommodating nature that adapts easily to a given situation,
> quickly forms attachments, and, setting aside any possible misgiv-
> ings, will often venture forth with careless confidence into unknown
> situations. In the first case obviously the subject, and in the second
> the object, is all-important.[416]

The crucial factor in determining whether one is introverted or extraverted, as opposed to which attitude is currently operative, is not
what one does but rather the motivation for doing it—the direction in
which one's energy naturally, and usually, flows.

Whether a person is predominantly introverted or extraverted only
becomes apparent in association with one of the four functions, each
with its special area of expertise: thinking refers to the process of
cognitive thought, sensation is perception by means of the physical

---

[415] "Psychological Typology," ibid., par. 986.
[416] "The Problem of the Attitude-Type," CW 7, par. 62.

sense organs, feeling is the function of subjective judgment or valuation, and intuition refers to perception via the unconscious.

Briefly, the sensation function establishes that something exists, thinking tells us what it means, feeling tells us what it's worth, and through intuition we have a sense of its possibilities.

> In this way we can orient ourselves with respect to the immediate world as completely as when we locate a place geographically by latitude and longitude. The four functions are somewhat like the four points of the compass; they are just as arbitrary and just as indispensable. Nothing prevents our shifting the cardinal points as many degrees as we like in one direction or the other, or giving them different names. It is merely a question of convention and intelligibility.
>
> But one thing I must confess: I would not for anything dispense with this compass on my psychological voyages of discovery.[417]

Jung's basic model, including the relationship between the four functions, is a quaternity, as shown in the diagram. (Thinking is here arbitrarily placed at the top; any of the other functions might be placed there, according to which one a person most favors.)

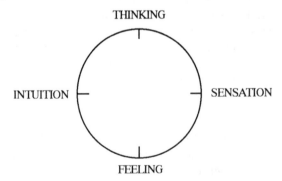

Jung believed that any one function by itself is not sufficient for ordering our experience of ourselves or the world around us; all four are required for a comprehensive understanding.

> For complete orientation all four functions should contribute equally: thinking should facilitate cognition and judgment, feeling

---

[417] "A Psychological Theory of Types," CW 6, pars. 958f.

should tell us how and to what extent a thing is important or unimportant for us, sensation should convey concrete reality to us through seeing, hearing, tasting, etc., and intuition should enable us to divine the hidden possibilities in the background, since these too belong to the complete picture of a given situation.[418]

The ideal is to have conscious access to the function or functions appropriate for particular circumstances, but in practice the four functions are not equally at the disposal of consciousness. One is invariably more differentiated, called the superior or primary function. The function opposite to the primary function is called the fourth or inferior function.

The terms "superior" and "inferior" in this context do not imply value judgments. No function is any better than any of the others. The superior function is simply the most developed, the one a person is most likely to use; similarly, inferior does not mean pathological but merely less used compared to the favored function. Moreover, the constant influx of unconscious contents into consciousness is such that it is often difficult for oneself, let alone an outside observer, to tell which functions belong to the conscious personality and which to the unconscious.

Generally speaking, a judging observer [thinking or feeling type] will tend to seize on the conscious character, while a perceptive observer [sensation type or intuitive] will be more influenced by the unconscious character, since judgment is chiefly concerned with the conscious motivation of the psychic process, while perception registers the process itself.[419]

What happens to those functions that are not consciously brought into daily use and therefore not developed?

They remain in a more or less primitive and infantile state, often only half conscious, or even quite unconscious. The relatively undeveloped functions constitute a specific inferiority which is character-

---

[418] "Psychological Types," ibid., par. 900. Jung acknowledged that the four orienting functions do not contain everything in the conscious psyche. Will power and memory, for instance, are not included, because although they may be affected by the way one functions typologically, they are not in themselves typological determinants.
[419] "General Description of the Types," ibid., par. 576.

istic of each type and is an integral part of his total character. The one-sided emphasis on thinking is always accompanied by an inferiority of feeling, and differentiated sensation is injurious to intuition and vice versa.[420]

Jung described two of the four functions as rational (or judging) and two as irrational (or perceiving).

Thinking, as a function of logical discrimination, is rational. So is feeling, which as a way of evaluating our likes and dislikes can be quite as discriminating as thinking. Both are based on a reflective, linear process that coalesces into a particular judgment. Sensation and intuition are called irrational functions because they do not depend on logic. Each is a way of perceiving simply what is: sensation sees what is in the external world, intuition sees (or "picks up") what is in the inner world.

Besides the primary function, there is often a second, and sometimes a third, auxiliary function that exerts a co-determining influence on consciousness. This is always one whose nature, rational or irrational, is different from the primary function.

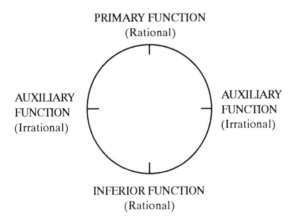

PRIMARY FUNCTION
(Rational)

AUXILIARY
FUNCTION
(Irrational)

AUXILIARY
FUNCTION
(Irrational)

INFERIOR FUNCTION
(Rational)

Jung's model of typology is the basis for modern type tests, such as the Myers-Briggs Type Indicator (MBTI) and the Singer-Loomis Personality Profile, used in organizational settings.

---

[420] "A Psychological Theory of Types," ibid., par. 955.

Unconscious. The totality of all psychic phenomena that lack the quality of consciousness. (See also **collective unconscious** and **personal unconscious.**)

> The unconscious . . . is the source of the instinctual forces of the psyche and of the forms or categories that regulate them, namely the archetypes.[421]

> The concept of the *unconscious* is for me an *exclusively psychological* concept, and not a philosophical concept of a metaphysical nature. In my view the unconscious is a psychological borderline concept, which covers all psychic contents or processes that are not conscious, i.e., not related to the ego in any perceptible way. My justification for speaking of the existence of unconscious processes at all is derived simply and solely from experience.[422]

The unconscious is both vast and inexhaustible. It is not simply the unknown or the repository of conscious thoughts and emotions that have been repressed, but includes contents that may or will become conscious.

> So defined, the unconscious depicts an extremely fluid state of affairs: everything of which I know, but of which I am not at the moment thinking; everything of which I was once conscious but have now forgotten; everything perceived by my senses, but not noted by my conscious mind; everything which, involuntarily and without paying attention to it, I feel, think, remember, want, and do; all the future things that are taking shape in me and will sometime come to consciousness: all this is the content of the unconscious.[423]

The unconscious also contains "psychoid" functions that are not capable of consciousness and of which we have only indirect knowledge, such as the relationship between matter and spirit.

Whenever the unconscious becomes overactive, it comes to light in symptoms that paralyze conscious action. This is likely to happen when unconscious factors are ignored or repressed.

---

[421] "The Structure of the Psyche," CW 8, par. 342.
[422] "Definitions," CW 6, par. 837.
[423] "On the Nature of the Psyche," CW 8, par. 382.

The demands of the unconscious then force themselves imperiously on consciousness and bring about a disastrous split which shows itself in one of two ways: either the subject no longer knows what he really wants and nothing interests him, or he wants too much at once and has too many interests, but in impossible things.[424]

In general, the compensating attitude of the unconscious works to maintain psychic equilibrium.

The unconscious processes that compensate the conscious ego contain all those elements that are necessary for the self-regulation of the psyche as a whole. On the personal level, these are the not consciously recognized personal motives which appear in dreams, or the meanings of daily situations which we have overlooked, or conclusions we have failed to draw, or affects we have not permitted, or criticisms we have spared ourselves.[425]

In terms of typology, the unconscious manifests through the opposite attitude and the less developed functions. In the extravert, the unconscious has a subjective coloring and an egocentric bias; in the introvert, it can appear as a compulsive tie to persons and things in the outside world.

Jung attributed to the unconscious a creative function, in that it presents to consciousness contents necessary for psychological health. It is not, however, superior to consciousness; its messages (in dreams, impulses, etc.) must always be mediated by the ego.

The unconscious is useless without the human mind. It always seeks its collective purposes and never your individual destiny.[426]

Consciousness should defend its reason and protect itself, and the chaotic life of the unconscious should be given the chance of having its way too—as much of it as we can stand. This means open conflict and open collaboration at once. That, evidently, is the way human life should be. It is the old game of hammer and anvil: between them the patient iron is forged into an indestructible whole, an "individual."[427]

---

[424] "General Description of the Types," CW 6, par. 573.

[425] "The Function of the Unconscious," CW 7, par. 275.

[426] *C.G. Jung Letters,* vol. 1, p. 283.

[427] "Conscious, Unconscious, and Individuation," CW 9i, par. 522.

Unconsciousness. A state of psychic functioning marked by lack of control over the instincts and **identification** with **complexes.**

> Unconsciousness is the primal sin, evil itself, for the Logos.[428]

> An extreme state of unconsciousness is characterized by the predominance of compulsive instinctual processes, the result of which is either uncontrolled inhibition or a lack of inhibition throughout. The happenings within the psyche are then contradictory and proceed in terms of alternating, non-logical antitheses. In such a case the level of consciousness is essentially that of a dream-state. A high degree of consciousness, on the other hand, is characterized by a heightened awareness, a preponderance of will, directed, rational behaviour, and an almost total absence of instinctual determinants. The unconscious is then found to be at a definitely animal level. The first state is lacking in intellectual and ethical achievement, the second lacks naturalness.[429]

> The greatest danger about unconsciousness is proneness to suggestion. The effect of suggestion is due to the release of an unconscious dynamic, and the more unconscious this is, the more effective it will be. Hence the ever-widening split between conscious and unconscious increases the danger of psychic infection and mass psychosis.[430]

Union of opposites. See **opposites.**

Unus mundus. See **coniunctio.**

Wholeness. A state in which consciousness and the unconscious work together in harmony. (See also **self.**)

> Although "wholeness" seems at first sight to be nothing but an abstract idea (like anima and animus), it is nevertheless empirical in so far as it is anticipated by the psyche in the form of spontaneous or autonomous symbols. These are the quaternity or mandala symbols, which occur not only in the dreams of modern people who have never heard of them, but are widely disseminated in the historical

---

[428] "Psychological Aspects of the Mother Archetype," ibid., par. 178.
[429] "Psychological Factors in Human Behaviour," CW 8, par. 249.
[430] "The Structure and Dynamics of the Self," CW 9ii, par. 390.

records of many peoples and many epochs. Their significance as *symbols of unity and totality* is amply confirmed by history as well as by empirical psychology.[431]

In terms of individuation, where the goal is a vital connection with the self, Jung contrasted wholeness with the conflicting desire to become perfect.

The realization of the self, which would logically follow from a recognition of its supremacy, leads to a fundamental conflict, to a real suspension between opposites (reminiscent of the crucified Christ hanging between two thieves), and to an approximate state of wholeness that lacks perfection.... The individual may strive after perfection ... but must suffer from the opposite of his intentions for the sake of his completeness.[432]

Will. The amount of psychic energy or libido at the disposal of consciousness, implying some control over instinct.

The will is a psychological phenomenon that owes its existence to culture and moral education, but is largely lacking in the primitive mentality.[433]

Wise old man. An archetypal image of meaning and wisdom.

In Jung's terminology, the wise old man is a personification of the masculine spirit. In a man's psychology, the anima is related to the wise old man as daughter to father. In a woman, the wise old man is an aspect of the animus. The feminine equivalent in both men and women is the Great Mother.

The figure of the wise old man can appear so plastically, not only in dreams but also in visionary meditation (or what we call "active imagination"), that ... it takes over the role of a guru. The wise old man appears in dreams in the guise of a magician, doctor, priest, teacher, professor, grandfather, or any person possessing authority.[434]

---

[431] "The Self," ibid., par. 59.

[432] "Christ, A Symbol of the Self," ibid., par. 123.

[433] "Definitions," CW 6, par. 844.

[434] "The Phenomenology of the Spirit in Fairytales," CW 9i, par. 398.

Word Association Experiment. A test devised by Jung to show the reality and autonomy of unconscious **complexes.**

> Our conscious intentions and actions are often frustrated by unconscious processes whose very existence is a continual surprise to us. We make slips of the tongue and slips in writing and unconsciously do things that betray our most closely guarded secrets—which are sometimes unknown even to ourselves. . . . These phenomena can . . . be demonstrated experimentally by the association tests, which are very useful for finding out things that people cannot or will not speak about.[435]

The Word Association Experiment consists of a list of one hundred words, to which one is asked to give an immediate association. The person conducting the experiment measures the delay in response with a stop watch. This is repeated a second time, noting any different responses. Finally the subject is asked for comments on those words to which there were a longer-than-average response time, a merely mechanical response, or a different association on the second run-through; all these are marked by the questioner as "complex indicators" and then discussed with the subject.

The result is a "map" of the personal complexes, valuable both for self-understanding and in recognizing disruptive factors that commonly bedevil relationships.

> What happens in the association test also happens in every discussion between two people. . . . The discussion loses its objective character and its real purpose, since the constellated complexes frustrate the intentions of the speakers and may even put answers into their mouths which they can no longer remember afterwards.[436]

Wounded Healer. An archetypal dynamic that may be constellated in an analytic relationship.

This term derives from the legend of Asclepius, a Greek doctor who in recognition of his own wounds established a sanctuary at Epidaurus where others could be healed of theirs.

Those seeking to be cured went through a process called incuba-

---

[435] "The Structure of the Psyche," CW 8, par. 296.
[436] "A Review of the Complex Theory," ibid., par. 199.

tion. First they had a cleansing bath, thought to have a purifying effect on the soul as well as the body. Uncontaminated by the body, the soul was free to commune with the gods. After preliminary sacrificial offerings, the incubants lay on a couch and went to sleep. If they were lucky, they had a healing dream; if they were luckier, a snake came in the night and bit them.

The wounded healer archetype can be schematized by a variation of the diagram used by Jung to illustrate the lines of communication in a relationship.[437]

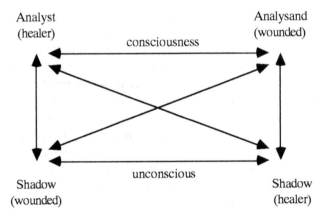

Analyst
(healer)

Analysand
(wounded)

consciousness

unconscious

Shadow
(wounded)

Shadow
(healer)

The drawing shows six double-headed arrows, indicating that communication can move in either direction—twelve ways in which information can pass between analyst and analysand.

According to this paradigm, the analyst's wounds, although presumed to be relatively conscious after a lengthy personal analysis, live a shadowy existence. They can always be reconstellated in particular situations, and especially when working with someone whose wounds are similar. (They are the basis for countertransference reactions in analysis.)

Meanwhile, the wounded analysand's inner healer is in the shadow but potentially available. The analysand's wounds activate those of the analyst. The analyst reacts, identifies what is happening

---

437 See "The Psychology of the Transference," CW 16, par. 422.

and in one way or another, consciously or unconsciously, passes this awareness back to the analysand.

In this model, the unconscious relationship between analyst and analysand is quite as important, in terms of the healing process, as what is consciously communicated. There are two other significant implications:

1) Healing can take place only if the analyst has an ongoing relationship with the unconscious. Otherwise, he or she may identify with the savior archetype, a form of inflation.

2) Depth psychology is a dangerous profession, since the analyst is forever prone to being infected by the other's wounds—or having his or her own wounds reopened.

> No analysis is capable of banishing all unconsciousness for ever. The analyst must go on learning endlessly, and never forget that each new case brings new problems to light and thus gives rise to unconscious assumptions that have never before been constellated. We could say, without too much exaggeration, that a good half of every treatment that probes at all deeply consists in the doctor's examining himself, for only what he can put right in himself can he hope to put right in the patient. It is no loss, either, if he feels that the patient is hitting him, or even scoring off him: it is his own hurt that gives the measure of his power to heal. This, and nothing else, is the meaning of the Greek myth of the wounded physician.[438]

---

[438] "Fundamental Questions of Psychotherapy," ibid., par. 239.

Bibliography

The Collected Works of C.G. Jung. 20 vols. Bollingen Series XX, translated by R.F.C. Hull, edited by H. Read, M. Fordham, G. Adler, and Wm. McGuire. Princeton University Press, Princeton, 1953-1979.

The names of the individual volumes are as follows:

1. Psychiatric Studies
2. Experimental Researches
3. The Psychogenesis of Mental Disease
4. Freud and Psychoanalysis
5. Symbols of Transformation
6. Psychological Types
7. Two Essays on Analytical Psychology
8. The Structure and Dynamics of the Psyche
9i. The Archetypes and the Collective Unconscious
9ii. Aion: Researches into the Phenomenology of the Self
10. Civilization in Transition
11. Psychology and Religion: West and East
12. Psychology and Alchemy
13. Alchemical Studies
14. Mysterium Coniunctionis
15. The Spirit in Man, Art, and Literature
16. The Practice of Psychotherapy
17. The Development of Personality
18. The Symbolic Life: Miscellaneous Writings
19. General Bibliography of Jung's Writings
20. General Index

C.G. Jung Letters. Bollingen Series XCV. 2 vols. Ed. Gerhard Adler and Aniela Jaffé. Trans. R.F.C. Hull. Princeton University Press, Princeton, 1973.

Memories, Dreams, Reflections. Ed. Aniela Jaffé. Pantheon Books, New York, 1961.

The Freud/Jung Letters. Bollingen Series XCIV. Ed. William McGuire. Trans. Ralph Manheim and R.F.C. Hull. Princeton University Press, Princeton, 1974.

Nietzsche's Zarathustra: Notes of the Seminar Given in 1934-1939. Bollingen Series XCIX. 2 vols. Ed. James L. Jarrett. Princeton University Press, 1988.

Index

Page numbers in **bold** type refer to a main entry

Studies in Jungian Psychology
by Jungian Analysts

Quality Paperbacks